SACRAMENTO PUBLIC LIBRARY
828 "I" Street
Sacramento, CA 95814
02/14

WIT
OF S

WITHDRAWN FROM COLLECTION
OF SACRAMENTO PUBLIC LIBRARY

D0123049

PROPERTY OF THE
OF SACRAMENTO PUBLIC LIBRARY

Also by Carol Berkin

Civil War Wives:
The Lives & Times of Angelina Grimké Weld,
Varina Howell Davis & Julia Dent Grant

Revolutionary Mothers:
Women in the Struggle for America's Independence

A Brilliant Solution:
Inventing the American Constitution

First Generations:
Women in Colonial America

Jonathan Sewall:
Odyssey of an American Loyalist

Wondrous Beauty

Wondrous Beauty

The Life and Adventures of
Elizabeth Patterson Bonaparte

Carol Berkin

Alfred A. Knopf New York 2014

This Is a Borzoi Book
Published by Alfred A. Knopf

Copyright © 2014 by Carol Berkin

All rights reserved. Published in the United States by Alfred A. Knopf,
a division of Random House LLC, New York, and in Canada by Random
House of Canada Limited, Toronto, Penguin Random House Companies.

www.aaknopf.com

Knopf, Borzoi Books, and the colophon are registered trademarks
of Random House LLC.

Library of Congress Cataloging-in-Publication Data
Berkin, Carol.
Wondrous beauty : the life and adventures of Elizabeth Patterson
Bonaparte / Carol Berkin.—First edition.
pages cm
ISBN 978-0-307-59278-1 (hardcover : alk. paper)
1. Bonaparte, Elizabeth Patterson, 1785–1879. 2. Jérôme Bonaparte,
King of Westphalia, 1784–1860. 3. Napoleon I, Emperor of the French,
1769–1821—Family. 4. Women—Maryland—Baltimore—Biography.
5. Baltimore (Md.)—Biography. I. Title.
DC216.95.B629B47 2014   943'.5506092—dc23   [B]   2013015270

Jacket image: Portrait of Elizabeth Patterson with her son, Jérôme
Patterson-Bonaparte (detail). 1806–1810. Attributed to François-Joseph
Kinson bpk, Berlin / Neue Galerie, Museumslandschaft Hessen Kassel /
Art Resource, NY
Jacket design by Kelly Blair

Manufactured in the United States of America

First Edition

To Eamon Joyce and Jessica Kumins Berkin

Contents

Introduction

She was a Baltimore legend, a curiosity, walking slowly down the streets of the city in the 1870s, her trademark red parasol high above her head to protect her from sun or rain or, in winter weather, draped carefully over one arm. On the other arm, she carried an ornate, elaborately embellished bag that, it was rumored, held all her jewels. Her dress was no longer fashionable, perhaps made in that bygone era when Napoleon dominated Europe and America was little more than a fledgling nation. No matter; it was clear she had once been a great beauty, and even in her old age, she conveyed an elegance and a sense of superiority that captured admiration as well as curiosity. As she stopped at one building and then the next, rapping on doors and demanding the rent owed to her by tenants, passersby might have recognized her as their city's first celebrity, Elizabeth Patterson Bonaparte.

Had those same passersby followed her home after her business was completed, they would have once again marveled at her eccentricity. Despite all the property she owned, both in the city and in surrounding areas, she abhorred the idea of setting up a household and had chosen to live in a rented room on the top floor of a stranger's home. The small room was crowded with ornate furniture, every surface covered with souvenirs, the single closet bulging with faded ball gowns that had been worn in the heady days after France's emperor was sent into exile. And there, in an atmosphere heavy with memory and nostalgia, they would have found her, poised to tell her story with the same wit and sense of irony and the same sharp powers of observation that had always been as much a part of her as her beauty and her ambition. She had lived a long and remarkable life—and she knew she had a remarkable story to tell.

Wondrous Beauty tells that story. It begins like a fairy tale of old: he was a dashing French naval officer who was the youngest brother of the great Napoleon Bonaparte; she was Baltimore's most beautiful belle, a seventeen-year-old eager to escape both the humdrum society of her native city and an overbearing father. They met. They fell in love as perhaps only teenagers then and now can do. Despite her father's serious misgivings and the French consul's blunt warning that Napoleon would not approve, Elizabeth Patterson and Jérôme Bonaparte married on Christmas Eve 1803. "We are not meant to be separate," Jérôme had declared—and yet they soon were. For there was no happily-ever-after to this romantic tale. In 1805, Napoleon annulled the marriage and sent the weak-willed Jérôme off to marry a German princess. Betsy, now the mother of an infant son, returned to America, an abandoned woman.

But if the fairy tale ended here, Betsy's story was just beginning. Her abandonment transformed her from a naïve girl into a fiercely independent woman. She refused to play the penitent, eager to make amends for poor judgment and youthful rebellion. Instead, when Napoleon was languishing on Elba, and his ban on her entering Europe was at last lifted, she crossed the Atlantic once again. She spent much of the next four decades in London, Geneva, Rome, and Paris. The celebrity she had once acquired in America because of her marriage was equaled by her celebrity in the ballrooms and salons of Europe; her tragic tale of betrayal, her beauty, her intelligence, and her wit proved as powerful a passport into the aristocratic society of the Old World as a wedding ring from Jérôme Bonaparte might have done. The belle of Baltimore became the belle of Europe.

Betsy never criticized the emperor who had destroyed her marriage. But she did not spare American society as she did Napoleon. Her stinging critiques of American mores and morals filled the pages of her letters home. She missed no opportunity to contrast the glamour and elegance of aristocratic European life with the pedestrian world of American shopkeepers and their wives. She condemned America as gauche and boring, its men too preoccupied with moneymaking to appreciate wit and good conversation, too democratic in their values to acknowledge the superiority of birth and breeding. Most of all, she condemned a gender ideal that demanded a woman's devotion to her husband and family, that confined her world to the parlor and the nursery, and that denied her the public space enjoyed by the women of the French salons. Even in her old age, when she had returned to her native city, Betsy continued to convey a certainty that she, no less than Henry Adams, was fated to remain a stranger in a familiar land.

Despite her efforts, Betsy could not instill in her son or his sons the same alienation from America and the same intense pride in carrying the Bonaparte name. For them, being the American Bonapartes proved as much a burden as a blessing. They embraced American culture and married American women—choices that Betsy read as betrayals as wounding as her husband's abandonment. As the Bonaparte fortunes fell and rose again in France, Betsy continued to cling to her dream that one day the American Bonapartes would take their place in that family's reviving power and privilege. This delusion was the burden she could not escape.

Perhaps Betsy's son and grandsons saw the ironic contradictions between her ideology and her behavior that she could not see. For despite her avowed distaste for American culture, she embodied many of its central values. She condemned her country's obsession with moneymaking, yet she proved to be a shrewd investor, carefully monitoring her assets, following interest rates and economic trends. She built a fortune based on government bonds and real estate that led to her emerging as a self-made woman in a world of self-made men. And although she exhorted her son to marry into the European nobility, she provided him with a Harvard education to ensure that he could make his way in the American meritocracy. Like expatriates in later generations, she carried American values with her no matter where she fled to escape them.

In the end, Betsy's story is a woman's story, for it captures the difficulty women of the early nineteenth century faced in constructing independent lives within a country that lauded self-interest and self-fulfillment for its men but confinement and sacrifice for their wives. What prompted her to cross the Atlantic Ocean was the promise of opportunities that an American woman could not hope to enjoy if she remained in her native land: intellectual freedom, the chance to establish an individual identity, and the right to exist not as a bundle of female duties or behaviors but as a unique person. She wished to be more than "female"; she wished to be Elizabeth.

Wondrous Beauty

Chapter One

"She Is a Most Extraordinary Girl"

Elizabeth Patterson Bonaparte's story began, as so many American stories still do, with an immigrant's arrival. The man who would become Elizabeth's father, William Patterson, was a perfect example of the economic opportunities the new republic promised and sometimes delivered. He arrived in Philadelphia in 1766, a penniless fourteen-year-old, a Scots-Irish castaway from that poorest of British possessions, Ireland. But what he lacked in education or family wealth, he made up for in raw ambition and keen business sense. As an apprentice in a countinghouse, he did not waste time, as many of his peers did, drinking or playing cards after hours; instead, he sought the company of older men, established merchants who could add to his knowledge of the buying, shipping, and selling of goods. He kept a keen eye out for the main chance, scrimping and saving while he waited for fortune to smile on him. His first good luck came in the form of the American Revolution.

William had no interest in enlisting in the army as many young men would soon do. Indeed, throughout his life he boasted that he had none of the civic pride that drove poor men to military service or rich men to philanthropy. As war approached, he wanted neither glory nor adventure. He wanted wealth and respectability. And he reckoned that a man who invested his money in the purchase and sale of European arms and ammunition could acquire both. At twenty-two, William Patterson risked his entire savings on shares in two vessels headed to France to purchase the weapons that the American army so desperately needed. Where his money went, William was determined to go as well, and thus the budding entrepreneur took passage in one of the ships.

On the return voyage, which carried the ships first to the West Indies, fortune smiled on William once again. Here, on foreign-owned islands like the Dutch St. Eustatius, military supplies could be warehoused before final sale and shipment to the American forces. A fine profit could be made for the middlemen in this process, and William meant to make it. His two ships sailed home, but Patterson remained in the Caribbean for eighteen months. With remarkable speed, his fortune grew, and so did his rejection of the risk-taking attitude that had begun his climb up the economic ladder.

In truth, by the age of twenty-five, Patterson had become that oxymoron, a cautious entrepreneur. He had worked hard to acquire his fortune, and he intended to keep it all. A strong fatalist streak ran through his philosophy: men could fall as quickly as they could rise, and the man who owned a mansion was only one foolish or impetuous step away from the beggar outside its doors. He did not plan to wind up on the outside looking in ever again.

By July 1778, William was ready to go home. But he did not head for Philadelphia; instead he made his way to the growing city of Baltimore, Maryland. Here, where he would live for the rest of his life, William began a pursuit of respectability and social status with the same steely ambition that had formerly marked his pursuit of wealth. Although his own parents had been Church of England, he joined the local Presbyterian church, for its pews were filled with the merchant elite of Baltimore. He built a fine brick home, and beside it he constructed his count-inghouse. He took a final step to the gentility he craved—and believed he had earned—by marrying Dorcas Spear, a beautiful young woman with impeccable family credentials.

In choosing Dorcas as his wife, William had not allowed sen-timent or affection to cloud his judgment. Despite the romantic revolution swirling around him that led genteel young men and women to seek a marriage built on affection and companion-ship, he saw wedlock as a simple matter of enhancing or consoli-dating economic or social advantage. What Dorcas thought of her new husband is unknown, for she left no record of her court-ship or of her own motives for the marriage. But it is clear that she was many things William was not: cultured, well educated, socially secure. Through blood and marriage, she was related to elite families in Virginia and Maryland, to revolutionary war officers and capital city political figures. And in temperament, she must surely have been patient and forgiving, for William proved a difficult man to live with and a faithless one at that.

By the time William and Dorcas said their vows, the bride-groom was numbered among the leading merchants and ship-pers not simply of Baltimore but of the new nation. He was intensely proud of his success, and it was a badge of honor that he was a self-made man. "What I possess," he declared, "is solely the product of my own labor. I inherited nothing of my forefathers, nor have I benefitted anything from public favors or appointments." His journey from rags to riches had come with a price, however. William's ambition, perseverance, and capacity for delayed gratification in everything but sexuality had calcified into a near obsession with security, a rigidity of thought, and a brittle sense of moral superiority. He valued practicality above sentimentality and found it easier to express disapproval than affection.

As a husband and a parent, William Patterson settled firmly into the role of patriarch. He expected not only obedience from all members of his family but also their confirmation of his wisdom in any situation. He was, in his own way, devoted to that family, but he could comprehend no other way to demonstrate his love than to control the lives of all who bore his name. He ruled his household with an iron fist that he believed to be a velvet glove.

William had strong, and unshakable, convictions about appropriate male and female roles in his family and in the larger society. For him, these roles were fixed and immutable. Men belonged in the broader public world of business and politics; women belonged in the home, where their lives were to revolve around the wishes and needs of husband or father. Other men might accept some latitude in the actual day-to-day compliance by their wives and daughters. Some might even delight in spirited or competent daughters as well as sons. But William was an absolutist. In this respect, he bore more resemblance to a fellow self-made man, a Frenchman named Napoleon, than to his American peers. "We treat women too well," the Corsican soldier would observe when he became emperor, "and in this way we have spoiled everything. We have done wrong in raising them to our level. Truly the Oriental nations have more mind and sense than we in declaring the wife to be the actual property of the husband."

Dorcas Spear Patterson would surely have disagreed with Napoleon that women were treated too well. Hers could not have been a happy life, for of her thirteen children, several died in childhood. And despite her submission to a domineering husband, she did not have the satisfaction of knowing that he honored his marriage vows. A string of mistresses, often drawn from the housekeeping staff, reflected his cavalier attitude toward marital fidelity; in 1814, as Dorcas lay dying, William would bring his current mistress into the household, no doubt to console him for the loss of a dutiful wife.

Dorcas's first daughter, Elizabeth Spear Patterson, was born on February 6, 1785. Elizabeth, or Betsy, and her country would grow up together, but from her earliest years, this child of the young republic would steadfastly refuse to embrace America's cultural and social trajectory. In part, this was the legacy of her mother's marital experience. The unhappiness that Betsy saw in the Patterson home seared into her consciousness the high cost of the social assumption that, in a proper household, a wife's duty was to please her husband and to spend a life confined to the parlor and the nursery. Betsy's devotion to her mother did not blind her to Dorcas's passive acceptance of her fate. She would carry a lock of Dorcas's hair with her all her life, but she would also carry her childhood memory of a woman bullied and scorned by her husband.

Dorcas had, however, played a second, more positive role in forging Betsy's rejection of American culture. For in her one rebellion against William Patterson, Dorcas Spear Patterson imparted to her daughter a deep appreciation of the arts, literature, and social refinement—an appreciation entirely foreign to her husband. Thus while others might find the vitality and expansiveness of the young republic exciting or satisfying, while they might praise the energy of its moneymaking or the fecundity of its women, Betsy came to see only a country that was raw and crass, devoid of any appreciation of high culture, its leading lights as dull-witted as its dock workers.

Betsy dreamed of an alternative, an escape from the culture into which she had been born. She found it, at least in her young imagination, across the ocean in the aristocratic world of Europe. Friends and neighbors, politicians and public opinion makers might condemn the Old World as stagnant and decadent, but in Betsy's vision, it was sophisticated and glamorous. Her romantic notions of the charms of Europe may have been fostered by the presence in Baltimore of a number of French émigrés and refugees, for the city's Catholic tradition acted as a magnet to Royalists fleeing the Terror, to displaced Acadians, and to the many white families uprooted by St. Dominique's slave revolts in the 1790s. The arrival of these French immigrants swelled the population of this Maryland port city and increased its prosperity. It also gave Betsy a glimpse of a culture very different from her own.

When she was ten, Betsy became far more familiar with the local French culture. That year her mother enrolled her at Madame Lacomb's school, where she mastered the French language. This fluency gave her entrée into the city's immigrant community. She formed a close relationship with Henrietta

Pascault, daughter of one of Baltimore's most cultured refugees, the Marquis de Poleon. For Betsy, the refined manners and sparkling sociability she witnessed in Madame's presence and in the Pascault household stood in sharp contrast to the somber atmosphere she found at home.

Indeed, for Betsy, the Patterson home was more prison than refuge. Her father watched over his children's lives with hawk-like concentration. He was unapologetic about his close supervision of everyone under his roof, including his adult unmarried sons. "I always considered it a duty to my family to keep them as much as possible under my own eye," he declared, "so that I have seldom in my life left home whether on business or pleasure." His rule, he added, was to "be the last up at night, and to see that the fires and lights were secured before I retired myself; from which I found two advantages: one was that there was little or no risk of fire under my own roof, and the other that it induced my family to keep regular hours." For William Patterson, sons and daughters, like lamps and fireplaces, were property under his care and supervision.

But of all his children, William believed Betsy was most in need of his watchful eye. Her yearning for an alternative to American society was only one of the traits that disturbed him. The truth was that this daughter was both a source of displeasure and an absolute mystery to William Patterson. He could not, and would never, see how similar in temperament and personality he and Betsy were; indeed, she shared with him a fierce ambition, a stubborn desire to have her own way, and in her teenage years, an impetuosity and risk-taking that reflected his own character at that same age. Father and daughter, so much alike, would spend their lives locked in a battle of wills that neither could hope to win.

Betsy found an escape from the pall cast by her father in books. She developed a habit of writing commentary in the margins as she read, and she would continue this in later years as she annotated the letters she read and saved. She was clearly precocious, memorizing French texts like La Rochefoucauld's *Maxims* and poring over a book by the French intellectual Madame de Staël. Her intelligence and intellectual bent did not escape the notice of more conventional friends and relatives. "She is a most extraordinary girl," observed another young Maryland woman, Rosalie Stier Calvert, labeling Betsy "in short, a modern *philosophe*."

Whatever the sources of her attachment to European culture—the French presence in Baltimore, the romantic poems and Enlightenment manifestos she read, her father's strict supervision, or her deep desire to escape her mother's fate—by the time she was seventeen, Betsy Patterson would have agreed with a later critic of American culture, Henry James, who would give voice to her discontent in succinct fashion: America lacked all that was desirable, "No sovereign, no court . . . no museums, no pictures." Betsy was convinced she had been born on the wrong side of the Atlantic. The problem was how to get to the other side.

Betsy's criticism of American culture and her attachment to Europe's aristocratic society made her unusual in Baltimore's elite circles. Her beauty made her exceptional. At seventeen, she was petite but perfectly proportioned; her hair was thick and chestnut brown; her eyes, which some described as hazel and others as blue, were large and bright. She was slender, with the softly rounded shoulders that men of her day admired, and her clear complexion was the envy of her female peers. Men were quick to take note of her extraordinary looks, and long into middle and even old age, she was showered with flowery compliments and ardent poetry from admirers. A young cousin declared in 1802 that even when she was absent, her beauty outshone that of other young women: "I most solemnly declare that all . . . were incapable of arresting my attention away for a moment—no madam each thought, each idea, were immoveably [*sic*] fixed upon the pleasing tho' dangerous, perhaps delusive contemplation of an absent object . . . at the bare recital of that name ten thousand inexpressible sensations crowd impetuously upon me."

Betsy was flattered but apparently unmoved by the admiration of local suitors. If she assumed, as surely all girls of her class and era did, that marriage and motherhood were an inevitable part of female life, she nevertheless nurtured a hope that someone would rescue her from the dull and constricting married life that lay ahead. And in 1803 that hope seemed to become a reality when a handsome stranger appeared in staid Baltimore City. His name was Jérôme Bonaparte, and he was the youngest brother of the first consul of France, Napoleon.

Jérôme was handsome, charming—and terminally spoiled. He was the youngest son of Letizia Ramolino and Carlo Buonaparte, who, like Dorcas and William Patterson, had thirteen children, although only eight survived. The family's rise was already legendary in 1803—from the isolation and unrest of Ajaccio, Corsica, to the slums of Marseilles and on to the palaces of France, where Napoleon now directed that country's political and military future. Carlos, who died when Jérôme was only an infant, had been extravagant and self-indulgent, but his widow, Letizia, was willing to sacrifice for her children. When Corsica was turned over to the French, she saw to it that they were educated in French schools. When the island's Italian population rebelled against French rule, she fled to the safety of Marseilles, where she took in laundry to support her younger children. Napoleon, already on his way to power, carried in himself Letizia's determination and focus; Jérôme, on the other hand, seemed to have inherited his father's hedonism.

As a child in Marseilles, Jérôme was not expected to contribute to the family's survival. While his older sisters and mother toiled as laundresses, the young boy played in the city's streets. Unlike his four brothers—Napoleon; the good-natured, intelligent Joseph; the gangly, nearsighted Lucien; and the often depressed and sexually ambivalent Louis—Jérôme was uneducated and undisciplined. Napoleon soon saw his brother for what he was, an illiterate street urchin, and set about to change him. It was too late: Jérôme had no interest in books, little intellectual rigor, almost no self-discipline, and no ambition except to enjoy the benefits, material and social, of being a member of the now great Napoleon's family.

Comfortably ensconced in Napoleon's palace, fourteen-year-old Jérôme quickly began to take full advantage of the first consul's wealth and fame. He ran up an impressive number of bills, all of which he ordered sent to his brother. Napoleon was stunned by Jérôme's profligacy. Nothing illustrated this irresponsibility and impulsiveness more than his young brother's purchase of an elegant and expensive travel set of shaving and grooming equipment—razors, shaving pots, mustache combs—all made of gold, silver, ivory, and mother of pearl. The cost—ten thousand francs—was shocking enough, but what caused Napoleon to fly into a rage was the fact that Jérôme Bonaparte was still too young to shave. When challenged, Jérôme replied that the absence of a beard was irrelevant; the shaving set was beautiful, and "I am like that: I only care for beautiful things."

Jérôme's character was thus formed: he was charming, irresponsible, self-indulgent. He loved beautiful things, and he soon discovered he loved beautiful women as well. If he was not willing to master science or math, he proved very willing to master the art of attracting women. He carefully studied the elite and elegant women who surrounded his sister-in-law Josephine de Beauharnais, and he recognized that, to win the hearts of such women, a man must be gallant, generous, and responsive to their wishes. To his natural charm, Jérôme therefore added the ability to read what a woman most desired—and to promise it to her.

Jérôme charmed many of the women who were assigned to oversee him. Indeed, Napoleon placed the blame for his younger brother's weakness of character on the women who spoiled him. "You brought him up well," he remarked sarcastically to Madame Permon, a woman blind to the boy's failings. "I find him willful, and willful in bad things." The greatest fault lay, however, with the matriarch of the family, Letizia Bonaparte, known as Madame Mère. As Napoleon knew, "Signora Letizia spoils him so totally that I much doubt whether he will mend."

In a final effort to cure Jérôme of his worst habits, Napoleon arranged a commission for his young brother in the French navy. He hoped that the rigors and discipline of military life would have a positive effect on the young man, and he hoped as well that, eventually, Jérôme's naval experience would be useful, as Napoleon determined a strategy for reducing England's domination of the seas.

Thus in 1803 the nineteen-year-old Jérôme was a naval officer, stationed in the Caribbean. His brother's influence ensured that he rose rapidly through the ranks. He moved in record time from midshipman to ensign to the commander of a patrol boat policing the waters around French-owned Martinique. When Jérôme's vessel encountered a ship that would not identify itself, the novice captain ordered his men to fire a warning shot across its bow. Unfortunately, the shot hit the rigging of the ship—an accident that had potentially serious consequences, as it turned out to be a British naval vessel. Jérôme's commanding officer, fearing the incident might disturb the fragile peace then existing between Britain and France and equally frightened that it might raise the ire of Napoleon himself, ordered Jérôme to sail home to France to explain things—at once. Jérôme, never good at taking orders he did not like, and worried that he might be captured by the British on the high sea, decided to ignore this order. Instead, he headed to the United States, traveling under the name M. d'Albert. His true identity was discovered soon after he landed on American soil.

Jérôme's arrival in America caused a stir, not simply because of his good looks, his flamboyant attire, and the impressive entourage of friends and servants who accompanied him. The

French chargé d'affaires in America, Louis-André Pichon, had no warning that the young naval officer had decided to visit the United States. He was astonished, he informed his superior, Talleyrand, to receive word that Jérôme had landed at Portsmouth, Virginia, and was on his way to Philadelphia to arrange transport to France. Without any instructions from Napoleon, Pichon did not know what to do. Jérôme suggested that Pichon ask the Americans to "lend him a frigate" or, if that were not possible, to allow him passage on the next American ship sailing to Europe. Both, as Pichon well knew, were out of the question: the United States was no more likely to "lend" one of its ships than it was to jeopardize its neutrality in the emerging Anglo-French struggle by allowing Napoleon's brother to sail under the American flag.

Jérôme decided to send one of his entourage, Lieutenant Meyronnet, to France with letters for the Bonaparte family. While he waited to hear their advice on his own travel home, he fell comfortably into the role of distinguished visiting dignitary. Having wrung a good deal of money out of the befuddled Pichon, he now decided to enjoy his time as a tourist.

One of the few Americans Jérôme knew was Baltimore's Joshua Barney, a larger-than-life sailor whose daring and bravery in the American Revolution had made him a local celebrity. Barney had begun trading with the French soon after their revolution and somehow encountered Jérôme in the Caribbean. The two men found they had much in common, especially their appreciation of the opposite sex. Barney had boasted that the most beautiful American women lived in Baltimore, and remembering this, Jérôme made his way to the Maryland port city. When the young Frenchman saw Elizabeth Patterson, he was ready to concede that Barney's boast was true.

Exactly how and where Elizabeth and Jérôme met is uncertain, for the accounts are many and various. According to one, Jérôme first saw Betsy while attending one of the Baltimore elite's favorite summer pastimes—a horse race. She was dressed in silk, and on her head she wore a hat decorated with ostrich plumes. But it was her face and form, not her elegant attire, that drew Jérôme's attention. What the writer of this account described as her "pure Grecian contours, her exquisitely shaped head, her large dark eyes, a peculiarly dainty mouth and chin, the soft bloom of her complexion, beautifully rounded shoulders and tapering arms" were perfection itself.

But there are other, equally romantic stories. They met, one account said, at a ball given by Supreme Court justice Samuel Chase. They were formally introduced, and Jérôme immediately asked Betsy for a dance. While they were dancing, Betsy's necklace became tangled in the buttons of Jérôme's uniform, a sign, it was said, that their lives too would entwine. Still another account has the two meeting at the home of her close friend Henrietta Pascault. As Jérôme and his friend Jean-Jacques Reubell came into view outside the door, Henrietta declared she would marry Reubell, the taller of the two. Betsy replied that she would marry his companion.

These accounts, with their images of instant attraction, their delight in young love, and their conviction that destiny had brought two exceptional people together, made their way into letters, memoirs, and newspaper accounts not only in Baltimore but throughout the United States. From her first encounter with Jérôme Bonaparte, Elizabeth Patterson became an American celebrity, and her fame would last until her death.

For Betsy, Jérôme's appeal ran deeper than his charm, his stylish dress, and the self-confidence that detractors saw as arrogance. In him she saw the antithesis of her dour and domineering father. And like the fairy-tale hero who rescues the imprisoned maiden from the tower, Jérôme could rescue Betsy from that life of tedious domesticity she feared was her future if she remained in America. For Jérôme, the attraction was far simpler, less fraught with meaning. Elizabeth was beautiful, and he longed to possess her, as he did any beautiful thing.

The meaning of their romance thus differed, and, so too did its expected consequences.

Though young, Jérôme Bonaparte had already enjoyed many romantic encounters, and no matter what promises he had made or what understanding he and his lovers had reached, marriage was not a likely outcome. But as he was quickly learning, the rules of courtship in genteel American society left little room for brief affairs. Indeed, even a quick embrace during a carriage ride—an action, Jérôme declared, that any Parisian woman would see as harmless flirtation—was read in America as an opening step to a marriage proposal. Betsy may have felt disdain for the domesticity that followed on the heels of marriage, but at seventeen, she was less a rebel against social norms than she imagined. She never doubted that she was about to become Madame Jérôme Bonaparte. And Jérôme decided he was willing to pay the price for possession of an object far more beautiful than ivory-handled razors.

Chapter Two

"I Would Rather Be the Wife
of Jérôme Bonaparte for an Hour"

In 1803 eighteen-year-old Elizabeth Patterson knew what she wanted: to be Jérôme Bonaparte's wife. Nothing else would do. "I would rather be the wife of Jérôme Bonaparte for an hour," she declared to her father, "than the wife of any other man for a lifetime." But William Patterson was not swayed by his daughter's dramatic declaration. In fact, he had serious doubts about such a marriage. Why would a French dandy pursue his daughter, and what were his real intentions? And if this romance did lead to marriage, what would the Bonapartes think of an alliance with an American family? William was naturally distrustful of this extravagant foreigner who spent money so freely, especially money that he had not earned. And he surely did not trust the judgment of an eighteen-year-old girl. William believed it was a father's duty to protect his daughter from her own foolishness, and thus, despite Betsy's pleas, he refused to give his blessing or permission for the marriage. Betsy's stubbornness matched his, of course, and before the summer ended, father and daughter had reached an impasse.

For his part, Jérôme was undaunted by Mr. Patterson's resistance. He mounted a campaign to win Betsy that was no less relentless than his brother's campaign to conquer Europe.

Using money Pichon provided, Jérôme rented a house on South Street, not far from the Patterson home. He then went boldly to William and asked for his daughter's hand in marriage. William refused. Next, Jérôme sent an emissary, the Spanish minister to the United States, to plead that the merchant reconsider his decision. Once again William refused. Jérôme persisted. He began to visit the Patterson family and brought his charming manner to bear on everyone from Dorcas to her three adult sons, William, Robert, and John; her two teenaged boys, Joseph and Edward; and even the four younger children, Margaret, George, Caroline, and Henry.

Although William grudgingly admitted that Jérôme conducted himself like a gentleman during his frequent visits, he was not prepared to relent. By September, a frustrated Jérôme decided to leave Baltimore and give William some time to think matters over once again. That month the rejected suitor headed off for a visit to Philadelphia. He remained determined to marry Betsy since this appeared the only way to possess her. Yet his behavior in the City of Brotherly Love made it abundantly clear that Jérôme Bonaparte's personal code of ethics, like William's, did not include fidelity. In Philadelphia, he amused himself by pursuing other women whom he found attractive. In one instance, his flirtation went too far, and he narrowly avoided a duel with an offended relative of the young woman. Fortunately for Jérôme, Betsy knew nothing of these flirtations. She knew only what he wrote in his letters—that he loved her and wanted her as his wife. She believed his every word.

Soon Jérôme was back in Baltimore. More confident than

ever that Betsy loved him, he decided to ignore William's reluctance. He acquired a marriage license from the local county courthouse and issued invitations to his wedding. At home, Betsy continued her own campaign to wring approval from her father. She was deaf to his words of caution, blind to any of the potential dangers that her father seemed to see so clearly. Despite her patina of sophistication, Elizabeth Patterson was, after all, a sheltered young American girl, her head filled with romantic notions of palaces and princes and a life so exciting that even her closest friends would envy her. Like other young women nurtured on romantic novels, Betsy was determined to overcome all obstacles put in her way.

Family members now joined the tug of war between William Patterson and his daughter. Her mother's family, the Spears, rallied to her cause. And Betsy's uncle, Senator Samuel Smith, supported her as well. Smith, however, was probably motivated more by thoughts of the economic and diplomatic advantages to be gained from an intimacy with the most powerful figures in France than by a wish to accommodate the personal desires of the young couple. His enthusiasm for the marriage increased when he considered how much his niece's marriage to a Bonaparte might improve his chances for an ambassadorship to France. William's firmest, and perhaps only, ally in the struggle to prevent the marriage was Louis-André Pichon. The French diplomat longed to see Jérôme safely on his way to France, for wherever Jérôme went in the United States, his bills came home to roost with Pichon.

Beleaguered from many sides, William slowly realized he was

losing ground. Betsy and Jérôme, sensing victory, proceeded with their plans for a November wedding. William now focused on protective measures, hoping to anticipate—and prevent— any disastrous consequences that might follow on the heels of the marriage. He saw to it that a prenuptial agreement was drawn up. It would protect Betsy in case marital problems arose, and, of course, it would protect any money William might settle on his daughter before the wedding. The terms of that marriage settlement were explicit and covered many contingencies. First, Jérôme would do all that was necessary to defend the legitimacy of the marriage, should any challenges arise in America or in France. Second, on Jérôme's death, one-third of his property both real and personal would be Betsy's. Third, if for any reason a separation occurred, Betsy's one-third share would still be valid. For his part, William guaranteed that, on his death, his daughter Elizabeth would receive a share of his very sizable estate equal to that of his other children.

But there were other dangers that a prenuptial agreement could not protect against. The marriage between the daughter of a prominent American merchant and a Bonaparte was not simply a private affair; it had, as Betsy's father well knew, political and diplomatic significance. As Secretary of State James Madison put it to the U.S. minister in France, the matter was "not without importance" at a moment when the struggle between France and Britain threatened the stability of the entire transatlantic world.

In fact, this proposed marriage could not have come at a more delicate juncture. The official position of the United States in the Anglo-French conflict remained neutrality. But "avoiding entangling alliances"—as Washington had urged in his farewell address—was proving difficult. The leadership of both the Federalist and the Democratic-Republican parties had to confront the challenge, for Americans were proving unwilling to give up the opportunities for trade or territorial expansion that the European conflict provided. In the 1790s, Federalist president John Adams had narrowly avoided war with France over a diplomatic slight known as the XYZ Affair, and the current Democratic-Republican president, Thomas Jefferson, would soon take drastic measures to avoid war with England over the impressment of American sailors and the confiscation of goods destined to France. And in the very year that Jérôme and Betsy were pressing for marriage, Jefferson was secretly engaged in delicate negotiations to purchase Louisiana from Jérôme's brother. The president hoped to succeed in this acquisition of a vast territory without any overt signs of support for France that could lead to war with England.

For his part, William Patterson had no desire to create an international incident by acceding to what he considered a daughter's foolish whim. For him, there were too many unanswered questions about the marriage: Would England interpret it as an overture to an American alliance with France? On the other hand, would any opposition to it by Napoleon be read as another French insult to the United States? Would influential Americans suspect William Patterson of reckless ambition? The possibility that his own business interests would suffer because of his daughter's impetuous step surely disturbed him.

William felt it his duty to protect his daughter, but he acted to protect himself as well. He asked his brother-in-law Sam Smith to secure letters of support for the marriage from President Jefferson and Secretary of State Madison. He wanted Smith to make it clear to all parties that he had done nothing whatsoever to promote or encourage the relationship between his daughter and the brother of Napoleon Bonaparte. But if and when the marriage did take place—and it now seemed to William inevitable—it should be presented to the Bonapartes as a socially acceptable alliance. American government officials agreed. In his instruction on the matter to the U.S. ambassador to France, Madison took care to emphasize that the proposed marriage was no insult to France's first consul's sense of self-importance, for it joined families of similar, if not equal, social rank. William would, no doubt, have been pleased to hear himself described as "a man of the fairest character, of real responsibility, [and] of very great wealth."

Still, not all of William's concerns were quieted. There was the question of Jérôme Bonaparte's age. Had he reached his majority, and was he thus able to marry without parental consent? Jérôme had not been forthcoming on answering this question. William assigned Smith the task of discovering the truth. When pressed, Jérôme reassured Smith that he had recently turned twenty-one. But whether Jérôme was twenty-one or several years younger than he declared, it might not matter. For Pichon informed Smith that a recent law in France declared that no marriage was valid without parental consent if the groom was under twenty-five.

This was a new twist. William set his lawyer the task of researching marital law. The lawyer reported that marriages were governed by the laws of the country in which they took place, and it was standard practice for such marriages to be accepted as binding in other countries. As Maryland set a man's maturity at twenty-one, Jérôme would need no parental consent. The lawyer seemed satisfied, but William Patterson was not. The moment the couple arrived in France, William realized, Napoleon or any member of the Bonaparte family, might—and under French law, could—challenge the marriage. In November, just as the wedding was to take place, he informed his lawyer that the engagement was off.

The danger of annulment by Napoleon was very real to William, but by November he had discovered other reasons for preventing the marriage. In his letter to the lawyer, Alexander Dallas, he had noted that "some circumstances of no great importance" had occurred the day before the ceremony was to take place. But those circumstances were far from inconsequential, especially to the father of a naïve daughter. For William had received an anonymous letter from someone who claimed to know Jérôme's true character.

The letter writer did not mince words. "Is it possible, sir," he or she began, "you can so far forget yourself, and the happiness of your child, as to consent to her marrying Mr. Bonaparte"? What followed was a litany of Jérôme's deceits and dissipations. He had "destroyed the peace and happiness of a respectable family in Nantz by promising marriage, then ruined, leaving her to misery and shame." The pattern had continued in the

West Indies, where he "ruined a lovely young woman who had only been married for a few weeks. He parted her from her husband, and destroyed the family!" As for Jérôme's motives for proposing marriage to Elizabeth Patterson, they were obvious: his brother Napoleon had gotten wind of this dishonorable behavior, and Jérôme "now wishes to secure himself a home at your expense" until his brother's anger cooled. When Napoleon forgave his errant brother, Jérôme would abandon William's daughter and "laugh at your credulity!"

William never knew who wrote this letter. He never knew if the accusations were true. But the warning resonated with his deepest suspicions and doubts. He would not allow Jérôme Bonaparte to humiliate his daughter—or to make a fool of her father. Exercising his parental authority, he whisked Betsy off to the countryside.

Betsy knew nothing of the anonymous letter, and thus for her, Jérôme remained the devoted lover who would ensure her happiness—and her escape from the stifling world of the Patterson household and the larger Baltimore society. She did know, however, that news of the cancellation of the wedding would spread quickly. Gossips noted that Betsy had been sent away; perhaps, as Rosalie Stier Calvert told her mother, she had been "driven off to one of her relatives in Virginia." Jérôme's whereabouts were no mystery: he had headed to New York. The young lovers were not able to communicate, yet someone kept Jérôme well informed of Betsy's whereabouts. Soon after she was allowed to return home, he appeared in Baltimore once again.

It was now clear to all that persistence had won out over prudence: the wedding was rescheduled for Christmas Eve. On the night before Christmas, a small group gathered at the Patterson home. Among the guests were Jérôme's personal secretary, Alexandre Le Camus; the mayor of Baltimore; and the French consul at Baltimore, M. Sotin. Louis-André Pichon, certain that Napoleon's wrath would soon descend upon him, did not attend. Although the Pattersons were Presbyterian, William had arranged for a Catholic ceremony, officiated by the highest of church officials, the Right Reverend John Carroll, first archbishop of America. Thus, in the eyes of the French Church, the marriage would be valid. And even if somehow the worst should happen, Article IV of the marriage contract, signed that very day, ensured that "if the marriage should be annulled, either on demand of the said Jérôme Bonaparte or that of any member of his family, the said Elisabeth Patterson shall have a right in any case to one-third of the real, personal and mixed property of her future husband."

At the ceremony, the bridegroom was resplendent in a coat of purple satin, embroidered and laced with gold. Diamonds sparkled on the buckles of his shoes, and his dark hair was powdered. But if Jérôme's appearance was a bit overwhelming, it was Betsy who created a stir. Jérôme had brought her a number of fashionable new dresses, bought during his stay in New York, but she chose to wear a simple muslin gown, decorated only with lace and pearls. It was shocking, not because of its simplicity but because beneath this sheer dress she wore only a single undergarment. As one guest described it, the bridal gown was little more than "a mere suspicion of a dress." There can be no doubt that the dress, which Betsy kept all her life, did not conform to the standards of propriety, as measured by multiple layers of undergarments and a near obliteration of the outline of the female figure. The dress may have reflected Betsy's delight in startling Baltimore's conventional community. Or it may only have been a sign that she had embraced the latest French fashions as eagerly as she had embraced a French husband. Unfortunately for her, that husband turned out to be only nineteen and thus was not old enough to marry, either in America or in France, without parental permission.

Chapter Three

"An Almost Naked Woman"

News of the wedding spread rapidly throughout the country, with announcements appearing in newspapers in Baltimore, Boston, Richmond, New York City, and Elizabeth, New Jersey. By February 1804, London papers were announcing that Jérôme and "the agreeable Miss Elizabeth Patterson" were married. Their social life as newlyweds was eagerly followed in the press and in private correspondence. Betsy was now a celebrity, and she proved more than happy to give everyone something to write about.

After a brief stay at one of the Pattersons' country estates, Betsy and Jérôme decided to make their way to Washington. Although the capital city was the hub of American politics, it was far from elegant. The distance between government buildings was often broad, and getting around could be challenging. Unpaved streets, muddy after rainfall or snow, were not passable on foot, and tree stumps often blocked the paths. Wildlife was abundant within sight of the Capitol. While a scattering of elegant homes housed elite members of the government, such as Secretary of the Treasury Albert Gallatin and the French minister, Pichon, many of the petty bureaucrats and office workers lived in rented rooms. Despite all the inconveniences, political figures and their families enjoyed balls and lavish dinners, evenings playing cards, and even the occasional theatrical performance. It was this active social life that attracted the young Bonapartes.

Washington City was only forty miles south of Baltimore, but even under the best of circumstances, the journey could be long and tiresome. In the winter of 1804, travel conditions were especially bad. Heavy snows blanketed Baltimore and the surrounding areas, and Washington itself was said to be bitterly cold. Jérôme rejected the idea of traveling by public stage; instead he borrowed Joshua Barney's personal carriage. Despite their comfortable transportation, the couple suffered an accident. The coach driver fell from his perch, the horses bolted, and though Jérôme attempted to take the reins and slow the horses' pace, the carriage went out of control. Betsy recognized the danger and, with considerable aplomb, jumped to the safety of a snowbank beside the road. She could, it became apparent, take care of herself when necessary.

It was not her bravery but a far different daring that made Betsy the talk of the capital. She set tongues wagging when she appeared at balls and dinner parties dressed in the latest European fashion. "Of Madame—I think it is no harm to speak the truth," wrote one Washington matron following a ball given in Betsy's honor. "She has made a great noise here and mobs of boys have crowded round her splendid equipage to see what I hope will not often be seen in this country, an almost naked woman."

Like Betsy's wedding dress, her ball gown was far more revealing than the older generation thought decent. It was made of thin, unstiffened white crepe, and thus it clung to her body, so "you could see the color and shape of her thighs." The dress had an empire waistline that, to another observer, was "scarcely any waist" at all. Betsy's arms, neck, and back were bare. In Paris, it was fashion; in America, it was indecent exposure.

To her critics, Betsy's attire reflected more than a lapse of one individual's personal morality or good taste. By 1804 fashion itself had become political. As the revolutionary fervor of the eighteenth century faded, a concern about the virtue necessary to sustain the republican experiment known as the United States grew. European decadence seemed to be creeping into American life, and although Jeffersonians laid the blame at the feet of the Federalists, it was a generational concern that crossed party lines. Would the recent effort to refine American society weaken it? Would American women, who had been designated as the torchbearers of patriotism and sacrifice, abandon their task of instilling these values in their sons and daughters? Modest dress was becoming the visible symbol of modesty in character—and Betsy's gown left her in every way exposed.

Betsy's embrace of Parisian and London fashion could also be—and was—read as a rejection of American domesticity. A woman who bared her neck and arms was surely a woman who would refuse to be a docile, obedient wife. Although Betsy was not alone among the younger generation in adopting the new foreign fashions, her appearance at social events on the arm of a Frenchman, and a Bonaparte at that, made the challenge to traditional manners and mores more disturbing.

Betsy's boldness both repelled and fascinated. Boys gawked,

and grown men were said to "take a look at her bubbies while they were conversing with her." Small wonder that one of the men at the ball penned a bawdy poem about her, declaring:

Well! What of Madame Bonaparte
Why she's a little whore at heart
Her lustful looks her wanton air
Her limbs revealed her bosom bare
Shows her ill suited for the life
Of a Columbian's modest wife

Betsy ignored the criticism, for at eighteen, she was not sophisticated enough to recognize the fine line that divided celebrity and notoriety. Her social triumphs were heady and made her deaf to criticism. She was proud of her new husband, eager to show off the Parisian fashions he had bought for her, and thrilled by the admiration she read in the eyes of men and the envy she saw in the eyes of women. When a delegation of older women warned her that "if she did not change her manner of dress she would never be asked anywhere again," she ignored them. She knew the threat was empty; all of Washington society clamored for a sight of the beautiful young woman some called "Lady Eve."

Not everyone disapproved of Betsy, of course. The portrait artist Gilbert Stuart, commissioned to paint Jérôme and Betsy, found her a living work of art. Seeing her, he decided to venture a composition he had never attempted before: three heads of a woman on one canvas. And Aaron Burr wrote to his daughter Theodosia Alston that Madame Bonaparte was "a charming little woman" who dressed with "taste and simplicity." Burr, who had raised Theodosia quite unconventionally, encouraging her to read widely and to think independently, approved of Betsy's "sense and spirit, and sprightliness." Meeting Betsy at a dinner party, Catherine Mitchill found her to be "remarkable friendly" despite her exposed "bubbies." She saw Betsy for what she was, vivacious and witty, with "a fondness to be heard." One could not expect such a sociable person to always be prudent, Mitchill declared, but she was very likely to always be amusing. It was to Catherine Mitchill, a sympathetic soul, that Betsy insisted that her sociability was nothing more than an antidote to misery and sorrow: "She says she is miserable, and is compel'd to fly to company for relief from sorrow." Mitchill seemed unconvinced, however. How could the young, beautiful wife of Jérôme Bonaparte need relief from sorrow?

Betsy might have been engaging in a bit of conversational melodrama, but she did have cause to suffer an underlying sadness. Her relationship with her father was intense, complex, contradictory, and never satisfactory. She defied him yet seemed always to desperately seek his approval. He criticized and condemned her yet felt frustrated that he could not protect her from others or herself. The battle of wills that became their most common mode of relating must have exhausted them both. But it was her father's infidelity that cut deepest, for it required Betsy to pity as well as love her mother. She saw Dorcas Patterson as a victim of social conventions but also, more than anything else, as a victim of a domineering and heartless husband.

In later years, she would write with bitterness and contempt of William's mistresses and his illegitimate child. Betsy's marriage to Jérôme held out the promise of escape from the stultifying culture of her native land, but it also promised escape from the unhappiness hidden from view within one of America's most prominent and stable families. She could not know, in 1804, that it would do neither.

Even if Betsy had dressed with the modesty that disapproving matrons demanded, controversy would have surrounded her. For in Washington, the presence of an American-born Bonaparte was certain to prompt political speculation. Did Betsy's marriage signal a shift in policy on the part of Jefferson's government? Jefferson fueled such speculation when he failed to give precedence to British ambassador Anthony Merry and his wife at a presidential dinner party, and he compounded the insult soon afterward, at another dinner, by escorting Betsy to the dinner table ahead of the wife of the British secretary of the navy. Whatever Betsy thought of the gesture, the Merrys believed its message was clear: the president of the United States had indicated his preference for France over England. Long after the excitement over Betsy's Paris fashions died down, Betsy's marriage would retain its political significance.

While Betsy and Jérôme enjoyed the social life of Washington and later New York, news of their marriage was making its way to Europe. The London *Times* carried the announcement, garnered from the New York papers, on February 4. Soon enough it traveled across the Channel. By February 18, Parisians could read that Jérôme Bonaparte had taken an American wife.

One of those reading the news was Napoleon Bonaparte. The first consul was not pleased.

The timing of Betsy's marriage could not have been worse. Jérôme had already taxed Napoleon's patience by abandoning his naval post and running up exorbitant bills everywhere he went, including the United States. Napoleon had read of the marriage only a few days after he sent Meyronnet back to America with orders that Jérôme return to France—at once. Even without this long list of sins committed by his youngest brother, Napoleon would have been in no mood to greet the marriage calmly. Jérôme's older brother Lucien Bonaparte had recently infuriated Napoleon by marrying his mistress, Madame Alexandrine Jouberthou, thus depriving the first consul of an opportunity to create a family alliance with one of the many noble houses of Europe.

Lucien had stood firm against his older brother. In a meeting with Robert Patterson, Betsy's brother, Lucien would later explain his refusal to bend to Napoleon's wishes. "When we marry we are to consult our own happiness and not that of another. It matters not who else is or is not to be displeased." Napoleon, however, did not see it this way. He considered the happiness of his brothers and sisters irrelevant; they must all bend to his wishes. His attitude was summed up by one of his ministers: "I owe nothing to my brothers . . . [but] they must not leave me isolated, and deprived of the aid and services which I have a right to expect from them." With her marriage, Betsy had successfully defied her father, a patriarch who expected his family to bend to his wishes as well; but unlike Napoleon, William did not have the power to create national law. Napoleon's *Code Napoléon* made it perfectly clear that no one under the age of twenty-five could legally marry without his parent or guardian's permission. It allowed Napoleon to dismiss the legitimacy of a ceremony conducted by an archbishop of the Catholic Church and witnessed by a member of his own legation. Betsy and Jérôme, he declared, were "no more man and wife than any other couple of lovers who united themselves in a garden, pledging their vows at the altar of love, in the presence of a witnessing moon and stars."

William Patterson was not present to hear Napoleon's outburst, but he already suspected that trouble lay ahead. Soon after the wedding, he had sent his son Robert to Paris to consult with the American minister and to test, as best he could, the reception likely to be waiting for the newest Madame Bonaparte in France. Robert arrived on March 11, 1804, and almost immediately received bad news. The American minister, trying to convey the degree of Napoleon's wrath, suggested that Jérôme and Betsy remain in America indefinitely. Lucien Bonaparte, who agreed to meet with Robert—and Robert's interpreter, the revolutionary war veteran Captain Paul Bentalou—was more encouraging. The entire family, Lucien said, with one unfortunately significant exception, was ready to welcome Elizabeth as Jérôme's wife. Nevertheless, considering who that exception was, he recommended that Jérôme stay in the United States and become a citizen there. As for Napoleon, he took no notice of Robert Patterson at all.

While Jérôme and Betsy continued their extended honeymoon, Napoleon mounted his attack on their marriage. He ordered his minister of the marine, Denis Decrès, to have Pichon inform Jérôme that the marriage was nonexistent—and, no doubt more serious for Jérôme, that all funds for his brother were to be cut off immediately. The captains of all French vessels were warned not to take aboard the "young person with whom Jérôme had entangled himself and should she attempt to enter France, she would not be suffered to land, but be sent immediately back to the United States." And before winter ended, Napoleon persuaded the French senate to pass an act forbidding any civil officer to even receive the transcript of the marriage. The senate's action reduced Betsy to a hapless participant in "a pretended marriage that Jérôme Bonaparte has contracted in a foreign country, during the age of minority, without the consent of his mother."

But all this bad news from France traveled slowly. In March, Jérôme could write to his mother that he was eager to introduce her to his "dear wife." It was not until April that he learned the legislature had labeled his marriage a sham. At about the same time, he received a long letter from Denis Decrès. Having been the lover of Napoleon's beautiful sister Pauline, the minister felt he had the right to send stern advice to Jérôme. He reminded the young Bonaparte that his country was once again on the brink of war and that his proper place was at his older brother's side. Honor and glory would come to family members who rallied to Napoleon, he wrote, but those who opposed him, like Lucien, would be cast out.

Jérôme was now uneasy, if not actually frightened. But he

gambled that, given time, Napoleon would relent. In this, he was sadly wrong. Napoleon, as fiercely proud of being a self-made man as William Patterson was, viewed himself as the "sole fabricator of my destiny." He owed nothing to his brothers; rather, they owed everything to him. He demanded their loyalty and obedience. Considering Lucien's marriage to be a betrayal, Napoleon did not hesitate to drive him into exile in Italy. If he could banish a brother who had long been a confidant and supporter, "what," he asked, "has Jerome to expect?"

Despite the bad news and dire warnings that came flooding in all at once, Jérôme's plan remained the same. He would sail to France on a French warship—*with his bride*—and introduce her to Napoleon. She would charm his brother—and all would be well. Toward this end, the couple, accompanied by Betsy's father, made their way to New York in June 1804. The Bonapartes boarded the *Didion* but were forced to disembark when British warships were spotted off the coast. Even had safe passage been possible, Betsy would have been left behind, for by this time, the captain of the *Didion* had received orders forbidding any French warship to allow her aboard. Learning this, Jérôme gallantly refused to board without her.

While they pondered what to do next, the young Bonapartes passed the summer in New York State, visiting Niagara Falls and enjoying the hospitality of New York City's social elite. By mid-August, they were back in Baltimore, still looking for safe transportation to France.

That September, Jérôme thought he had arranged suitable travel. Bowing to reality, he now agreed to go alone on a French frigate while his wife made the journey on an American vessel. Her escort would be the new American minister to France, General John Armstrong. But once again the plan fell through. Finally in October, Jérôme, Betsy, and her chaperone, her aunt Nancy Spear, boarded an American merchant vessel at Philadelphia. Before they could reach the ocean from Delaware Bay, however, the ship was destroyed by a violent storm and the passengers had to leap from the deck to a lifeboat below. Newspaper accounts claimed Betsy was the first one to jump. Wet and cold, they took refuge with a family living along the bay. Although Miss Spear thought the proper thing to do was to kneel and thank God for their safe delivery, Betsy considered her survival a matter of personal bravery rather than divine intervention. Rather than prayer, she preferred to celebrate by eating a hearty meal. That December the Bonapartes tried once again to make the transatlantic crossing. But once again British warships blocked their way. There could be no more attempts until spring.

Betsy and Jérôme had failed to reach France, but Napoleon had succeeded in taking that country over completely. On May 18, 1804, Jérôme's older brother declared himself emperor. After his coronation in the Cathedral of Notre-Dame that December, the new ruler of France began to distribute rewards and honors to members of his family whom he considered deserving. Brothers Joseph and Louis were made princes of the empire and Napoleon's successors should he die without a son. Joseph was soon named king of Naples and Louis king of Holland. Even sister Caroline's husband, who began life as an innkeeper's son, would now be called Prince. Noticeably absent from the new emperor's honor roll were Lucien and Jérôme. When Jérôme learned of these events in late February 1805, he surely began to realize the high price he had paid for love.

At last, in March 1805, William Patterson took matters into his own hands and chartered a ship to carry his daughter and her husband across the Atlantic. The *Erin* was sleek and fast, able to outrun any British ship hoping to enforce the blockade. William also provided the couple with funds and provisions for the journey. When they were not laid low by seasickness, Jérôme, Betsy, and their entourage—including Jérôme's physician and Betsy's oldest brother, William Jr.—passed their days playing cards, games, and backgammon. If Jérôme's thoughts turned frequently during their long voyage to his first meeting with the emperor, Betsy's may have been on more intimate concerns. She was six months pregnant, and there would soon be a new Bonaparte in the emperor's family.

Chapter Four

"Have Confidence in Your Husband"

Although the seas were rough, the voyage to Europe was mercifully swift. On April 2, after only a little more than three weeks, the *Erin* reached Lisbon with Betsy, Jérôme, William Patterson Jr., Betsy's friend Eliza Anderson, Jérôme's doctor, and his secretary, Alexandre Le Camus, on board. It was here that Betsy learned how thoroughly unwelcome she was in Napoleon's Europe. She was allowed to go sightseeing and shopping with her husband but not to travel any farther with him. The message could not have been clearer, but Napoleon added insult to injury: he was willing to pay her off if she would go away quietly. When his messenger explained that Napoleon was willing to provide her with a pension if she promptly returned to America and gave up the Bonaparte name, Betsy snapped back: "Tell your master I shall never relinquish a name he has made so famous. . . . Tell him that Madame Bonaparte is ambitious and demands her rights as a member of the imperial family." Her reply was both a challenge to Napoleon and a sign of her admiration for his achievements. She would not be bought off; she would not trade prestige and reflected glory for mere money.

Jérôme tried to soothe Betsy's injured pride and calm her growing anxiety by purchasing a set of garnet jewelry for her.

On the clasp of the bracelet, he had the jeweler engrave a single word: *Fidelité.* Then he said his goodbyes, for he had been ordered to come at once to Napoleon, and he thought it best to obey. Amid promises that they would soon be reunited and that all would be well, Jérôme left for a rendezvous with the emperor. On April 9, some four days after he departed, Betsy recorded in her notebook, "Mon mari est parti de Lisbon." She would not see him again until they passed each other in the gallery of the Pitti Palace in Florence, decades later.

Jérôme was headed to Italy to see his brother. Betsy and her traveling companions aboard the *Erin* now headed to the Netherlands, where they hoped Napoleon's ban might not apply. The weather at sea was terrible, and this voyage took twenty-six days. By the time the ship reached the Texel River, provisions had run dangerously low and the drinking water was almost gone. But the Netherlands proved no haven. Their greeting was a warning shot fired at them by a battleship. Within a short time, the *Erin* was hemmed in by warships. Realizing he could not make port, the captain sent a plea for supplies. The request was ignored until several days later, when the port commander relented and sent food, water, wine, and liquor. But he also sent an order: leave immediately. On May 17 the *Erin* set sail again, this time for the only country likely to welcome them: England.

Jérôme apparently knew nothing of his wife's difficulties. Soon after he departed, he sent a letter, addressed to her at Lisbon. His tone was, as always, reassuring. "The worst thing that could happen to us," he declared, "would be to live quietly abroad, but when we are together aren't we certain to be happy?"

By April 19, he learned she had headed to Amsterdam. He wrote to her there, addressing the letter to "Madame d'Albert," using the same alias he had used on his arrival in America. He assured her that before June ended, he would join her there. "I must do my best with my brother," he added. "He is my Emperor and has always been a tender father to me. But after I have done my duty and have nothing to reproach myself with I will live, if it be necessary, withdrawn with my little family in no matter what corner of the world."

Jérôme's "tender father" was far from ready to forgive him, however. In a letter to their mother, Letizia, the emperor had made it clear that Jérôme must be "disposed to wash away the dishonor with which he has soiled my name in abandoning his colors and his ship for a miserable woman." If the younger Bonaparte failed to make amends, Napoleon intended to "give him up forever" and, more ominously, make an example of him. Napoleon's ire was immediately evident to Jérôme, who was left to cool his heels outside Napoleon's headquarters. When Napoleon at last agreed to an audience, he was said to greet Jérôme coldly: "So, sir, you are the first of your family who shamefully abandoned his post. It will require many splendid actions to wipe that stain from your reputation. As to your love affair with your little girl, I do not regard it."

Napoleon's threats had not worked on Lucien, who stood by his wife despite exile and accusations that he had betrayed the emperor. But Jérôme lacked his older brother's strength of character. As Napoleon heaped threats upon him—no more funds, no place in the line of succession, no honors, no glory, no royal title, and the possibility of court-martial—Jérôme's resolve, if it had ever truly existed, evaporated. On May 6, as the *Erin* tossed on rough seas toward Amsterdam, Betsy's husband capitulated completely to Napoleon.

The *Erin* reached Dover on May 19. Betsy discovered when she disembarked that her plight had made her a celebrity in England, just as her marriage had made her a celebrity at home only a few years earlier. Crowds gathered at the dock to catch a glimpse of the young, pregnant woman whom Napoleon had driven from the shores of Europe. But here, as in Washington City, her critics were as numerous as her supporters. British popular opinion was divided: Was she a sympathetic victim of a cruel tyrant, or was she a collaborator with that tyrant who had been cast aside? The newspaper reports captured this ambiguity. In its account of Madame Bonaparte's arrival, the London *Times* quipped, "She appears far advanced in a situation to increase the number of Imperial relatives." The sarcasm was aimed as much at Betsy as at Napoleon.

If the press was willing to criticize Betsy as readily as it was to romanticize her plight, the British government was far more careful to present itself as a reliable friend. Betsy was, after all, a valuable asset in the propaganda war to win support from the United States. Thus Prime Minister William Pitt sent a company of soldiers to escort and protect her from any unpleasant jostling by the gawking crowd. The minister hoped that English kindness and consideration would provide a stark contrast to the insulting behavior of Napoleon. Patriotic newspapers were quick to point out this contrast, declaring that Betsy, who had suffered humiliation at the hands of "the Imperial Swindler" and his contemptible brother Jérôme, was now safely "under the protection of a great and generous people."

Betsy surely appreciated Pitt's assistance. She was exhausted, physically and emotionally, and more than seven months pregnant. She was also far more politically savvy than she had been in the earlier days of her marriage. She knew that the British government's readiness to use her situation for diplomatic ends would raise Napoleon's ire. Any public attention, especially if it was friendly, had to be avoided. With crowds gathering daily for a glimpse of her in London, Betsy sought refuge in the quieter surroundings of Camberwell, England. There, on the morning of July 7, 1805, she gave birth to a son. She had the presence of mind to ensure that there were witnesses present and that the infant's birth certificate was notarized. In naming her child, she linked together the two Frenchmen who held her fate in their hands. He was called Jerome Napoleon Bonaparte.

Betsy had found a safe haven in England, but her future remained clouded. She had received no word from Jérôme since they parted in Lisbon, for the letters he had written had missed her, both in Portugal and in the Netherlands. Even if he had known where she was, it would have been risky for him to try to communicate with her, or to try to send word to her through trusted friends. Napoleon was quick, in fact, to punish anyone who helped Betsy or the Pattersons. The emperor had jailed Paul Bentalou for his role as an interpreter when Robert Patterson spoke with Lucien Bonaparte. Jérôme feared that Napoleon's spies were watching him and that any sign of a breach in his capitulation to the emperor's wishes would carry serious consequences. Sometime in mid-May Jérôme risked sending a letter to Betsy, but it did not reach her for several years. Then Jérôme attempted to send word to Betsy through the Dowager Marchioness of Donegal, but it took this go-between six weeks to discover where Madame Bonaparte was residing.

For her part, Betsy had no idea how to contact her husband. English newspapers reported that he had been reinstated in the French navy and was already at sea. A letter she wrote to Bentalou went unanswered. Another, to the daughter of the U.S. ambassador to France, Elisa Monroe—asking, "Would it be asking too much to request you would sometimes write me to communicate what occurs"—received no reply. A note to Lucien Bonaparte, pleading that he convey a simple message to Jérôme—"Please let me know your intentions concerning myself and your child"—was met with silence. She did receive a letter dated July 15 from Jérôme's physician and her former shipmate, Dr. Garnier. According to the doctor, Jérôme was deeply distressed about her suffering but was even more distressed that she had sought refuge in the land of France's enemy. Her husband, Garnier continued, instructed her to return to America as soon as possible. But, as Betsy later wrote to her father, she did not trust anything the doctor said; his letter "bears all the marks of being a deception."

Betsy had no reason to mistrust the Marchioness of Donegal when, at long last, the dowager located her. It was possible, Betsy thought, that the marchioness could serve as her much-needed line of communication with Jérôme. Writing to the noblewoman on August 14, 1805, Betsy took pains to stress her willingness to comply with any instructions Jérôme might give. "Will you then have the goodness to inform Mr B—thro' the same channel, that I will act with implicit obedience to his wishes as to the place of my residence & with respect to every thing else he desires." Aware that Dr. Garnier's report that Jérôme was angered by her decision to take asylum in England might be true, Betsy added an explanation: "I sought refuse [*sic*] in England not from any particular predilection for it but on my being refused admittance at Amsterdam my situation (being at that time far advanced in pregnancy) obliged me to seek an asylum in any country where I could be received." Since her arrival, she added, she had taken care to live "in the most secluded retirement 3 miles from Town. I avoid every thing that can excite observation or comment . . . & . . . I will never act otherwise than with the propriety that my own dignity & that of his wife require." She closed the letter with the hope that the marchioness would convey to Jérôme her "firm conviction of his sincerity & honor." She would learn soon enough that Jérôme's "honor" had failed her. He had already renounced her, as part of his reconciliation with his older brother.

Despite Jérôme's abandonment of his wife, his friends took pains to assure the Pattersons that he was suffering greatly from their separation. Alexandre Le Camus conceded to William that Jérôme must, for the time being, bow to his brother's wishes. But, he added, there was still hope that Napoleon would relent if Jérôme proved himself in an upcoming naval mission. "Your daughter," he declared, "has only to yield to the present, and expect a better time." William must have been unconvinced, for he did not bother to convey Le Camus's advice to his daughter.

About three weeks after Jerome Napoleon Bonaparte was born, his father risked a second letter to Betsy. It was filled with declarations of love, justifications for his actions, and calls for patience and understanding. "You know with what regret I left you at Lisbon," he wrote, "and God, who sees into my heart, knows that I live and breathe only for my wife." He urged her not to believe any accounts of what had transpired in his talks with Napoleon. He alone could—and would—tell her the truth. Meanwhile she should not judge Napoleon harshly, and above all she should be patient. "My brother is as good and as generous as he is great, and if political reasons force him at present to this conduct, the day will come when that will change." He closed with assurances of his own devotion: "Have confidence in your husband, be convinced that he breathes, dreams, works, only for you, yes, for you alone and our child. . . . I kiss you a thousand times, I love you more than ever."

As he penned this letter to Betsy, it is likely that Jérôme believed every word was true. Acquaintances who saw him at the time were touched by his melancholy and noted that he spoke often of "my dear little wife." But it is difficult to know if the air of dejection he wore stemmed from his failure to get his way with his brother or from a genuine and mature commitment to his wife and child. That he filled a letter with emphatic exclamations of devotion and pledges of undying love tells little; for a young man of Jérôme's accommodating nature in dealing with women, this was the only possible way to speak to his beautiful wife. The circumstances called for romantic declarations and firm reassurances, and Jérôme delivered both with the sincerity of a callow youth. The truth was, he had already recognized that he had more to lose if he disappointed his French emperor than his American wife.

This letter did not reach Betsy while she was in England. All through the fall and winter of 1805, she remained in the dark about both her husband's intentions and his whereabouts. Jérôme had, in fact, written her several letters that fall, each filled with the same sentiments that he had expressed in the missing letter, but she received none of them. Believing now that she was abandoned, Betsy canceled plans to remain in England through the winter. She would return to Baltimore with her brother Robert and her infant son. Just as she was preparing to leave, several boxes arrived from France containing dresses, hats, jewels, a miniature of Jérôme—and gold pieces worth almost fifteen hundred dollars. These were the last extravagant signs of affection she would receive from her husband.

On November 14, 1805, after six weeks on stormy seas, Betsy Patterson Bonaparte arrived home. Her mother and her many siblings were eager to greet her and her young son. But the welcome she received from her father was far less warm. William could not measure the emotional cost of Betsy's abandonment, but he knew to the last penny the financial cost of her romantic escapade. For William had saved every receipt for his expenditures, from the outfitting and provisioning of the *Erin,* to Robert's Paris expenses, to the funds he had made available for her on the continent, and to those she had used in England. Time as well as money had been wasted, for Robert and William had been absent from the family business for months. Even more infuriating, Betsy's erstwhile husband had left Baltimore in debt to local shopkeepers, tailors, stable owners, and shoemakers and William felt honor-bound to pay these bills. In America as in France, Jérôme left it to others to pay for his extravagances.

William clearly felt all this could have been avoided if Betsy had obeyed him in the first place. He had opposed the marriage; he had tried his best to prevent it. In the end, he had surrendered to his daughter's unshakable confidence in her own charm, and given way to her stubborn conviction that Napoleon would succumb to her beauty and wit as other men had so often done. He had, he believed, financed a fool's errand and now bore the real burden, the dollars-and-cents burden, of her stubborn disregard for paternal authority. If he could not change the past, he was determined to recoup what he could from the present. When the boxes containing Jérôme's last gesture of generosity arrived from London, William claimed half the gold that his former son-in-law provided. He was not content to stop there. As Betsy recorded, her father "sold to his own profit horses, carriages, serving to furnish his house at Cold Stream with plate, china, glass, tables, carpets, chairs, beds, etc etc, all that had been left at Baltimore by his imperial son-in-law."

Betsy was enthusiastically welcomed back into Baltimore society, but given William's obvious anger, she remained uncomfortable in her father's home. His certainty that Jérôme had played her for a fool weighed heavily on her already fragile morale. Through the early months of 1806, as Jérôme's letters of 1805 followed their circuitous path to Betsy's doorstep, she struggled to maintain some hope that her husband would prove her father wrong. In April she received the notes of assurance that he had sent from Paris six months before. Then in May she received a letter written while he was on naval duty. In it, he expressed resentment that his sincerity had been doubted. If I intended to abandon you, he wrote with obvious indignation, I would already be sitting on a throne somewhere in Europe. Instead, I am aboard a ship, serving my emperor.

This letter made Betsy wonder if she had indeed misjudged Jérôme. Was he loyal to her after all? Perhaps as he had always insisted, Napoleon would relent if his young brother acquitted himself honorably in the naval battles being waged against Britain. Her optimism was intense, but it was short-lived. By June the tone in the letters coming from Jérôme had changed dramatically. Assurances had turned to accusations. He laid all blame for their situation at her feet. "Your departure for England," he declared, "was the only cause of our separation." The signature on the last letter she received revealed his clear change of heart: the impersonal closing, "J. Bonaparte," told Betsy that the marriage was indeed over.

Jérôme's confidence that Napoleon would eventually forgive him proved correct. But Betsy would not reap the benefits of the emperor's renewed affection. While she was wrestling with the meaning of her husband's promises and then his rejection, a placated Napoleon was busily trying to arrange a suitable new marriage for his youngest brother. The emperor's victories against a coalition of Britain, Austria, Russia, Sweden, and several German states had expanded his empire across much of Prussia, Germany, Austria, and Italy, and he intended to place men he could trust in positions of power in the newly acquired areas. Marriage between his brothers—or sisters—and local leaders was thus a useful strategy. If Lucien had refused to cooperate, Jérôme's resistance to Napoleon's will now seemed broken. After two proposed matches failed in 1806, Napoleon finally hit upon a perfect arrangement: he would marry Jérôme to the daughter of the new king of Württemberg.

The king, who owed his title to Napoleon, had the temerity to express his concern that Jérôme was, in fact, already married in the eyes of the church. Napoleon acted quickly to remedy the problem. He appealed to Pope Pius VII to annul his brother's marriage, claiming that there was danger in having a Protestant in close proximity to a Catholic emperor. The pope was not persuaded that a young woman posed a serious threat. When Pius refused Napoleon's request, the French ruler took matters into his own hands. He pressured the Parisian ecclesiastical court to do what the pope would not. By October 1806, the marriage of Jérôme Bonaparte and Elizabeth Patterson had been invalidated.

All was thus in readiness when Jérôme arrived from his string of successful naval missions in the Atlantic. The former deserter was now pronounced a national hero, and Napoleon heaped rewards on him. Jérôme was made a rear admiral and a prince of the realm, a man to be addressed as "royal highness." Jérôme's elation was only slightly diminished when Napoleon broke the news to him that he was to be a husband once again.

While Jérôme reveled in his newfound prestige, Betsy was in Washington, visiting her aunt and reestablishing social connections with Dolley Madison. Dolley, who shared Betsy's love of fashionable clothes and sparkling dinner conversation, served as the widowed Thomas Jefferson's hostess at all presidential social events. This made her the undisputed leader of Washington society. Like so many of Betsy's personal decisions, her close association with Dolley seemed to carry political implications. Jefferson's pro-French—or more accurately, his anti-British—sentiments were well known; did the two women's friendship suggest that Betsy, too, had cast her lot with the French? The Federalists were appalled; how could she ignore the implicit insult to American honor contained in the emperor's dissolution of her marriage? But it was Betsy's refusal to condemn Napoleon, whose power and ambition she would admire for the rest of her life, that ensured her private crisis would continue to have political overtones.

It was in Washington that Betsy began to hear the rumors of Jérôme's proposed marriage to the princess of Württemberg. Soon enough she also heard rumors that her own marriage had been annulled; although it was not unexpected, the news, if true, was a terrible blow. Both rumors, of course, proved correct. On July 7, 1807, Napoleon rewarded Jérôme's loyalty with a kingship. The emperor had been revising the map of Europe, carving new countries out of conquered areas of Prussia and Germany. One of the new kingdoms was tiny Westphalia, lying to the east of Belgium. Jérôme would wear the Westphalian crown. His queen would be Princess Catherine Fredericka Sophia Dorothea of Württemberg.

Jérôme was unlikely to feel the rush of desire to possess his queen-to-be that he had once felt for Betsy Patterson. Nineteen-year-old Catherine was neither pretty nor charming, although she proved herself to be kind and caring during their long marriage. She was short, without the long neck that signaled grace and beauty in the Napoleonic era, and she rarely smiled. The Duchesse d'Abrantès, who believed Jérôme regretted his divorce but simply did not have the "strength of mind" to resist the pressures put upon him, described the poor impression Catherine made on her first meeting with him. The *duchesse,* who was present at the first meeting of the young couple, expressed regret "that no one had the courage to recommend her a different style of dress." Instead, Catherine wore a gown "in a style which had . . . been forgotten . . . with a train exactly resembling the round tail of the beaver." The meeting was brief; after a short conversation, Jérôme announced, "My brother is waiting for us," and left the room. Catherine realized the meeting had gone badly. "The colour in her cheeks increased so violently," the *duchesse* wrote, "that I feared the bursting of a blood-vessel." Then Catherine fainted. Despite Jérôme's lack of enthusiasm for his future wife, their wedding took place on August 12, 1807.

Jérôme filled the weeks and months that followed running up bills that quickly drained the Westphalian treasury. In addition to his own dazzlingly extravagant wardrobe—including satin suits embroidered with gold—he dressed members of his palace staff in velvet capes. He was soon borrowing money to cover his debts. Napoleon watched with disgust. Although he spoke bluntly to Jérôme, declaring, "I have seldom seen anyone with so little sense of proportion as yourself," he knew the censure fell on deaf ears. His younger brother was simply beyond reform. "Jérôme," Napoleon told a confidant, "cares for nothing but pageantry, women, plays, and fêtes." But no matter how harshly Napoleon criticized him, Jérôme remained confident that he would eventually be forgiven. In the end, it was Catherine who did most of the forgiving, for Jérôme was regularly, and flagrantly, unfaithful to his wife.

While Jérôme was refurbishing royal buildings and appointing incompetent friends to positions of responsibility, Betsy was rebuilding her own life. What might have seemed an ending for an early-nineteenth-century American woman abandoned with a small child was, for Betsy Patterson Bonaparte, only the beginning. Her prince charming had failed her, but she was now ready to create a fairy-tale life for herself.

Chapter Five

"Madame Bonaparte Is Ambitious"

A lthough at twenty, Betsy was still young and beautiful, by 1805 she was no longer naïve. She had grown cynical, and over the coming years, she would come to share with her father that distrust of other people's motives that was the darker side of self-reliance. For the moment, however, it was enough that she was determined to find her own voice, to make her own decisions. She would no longer rely on her father or brothers to protect her interests, and thus she would no longer have to justify her choices. She would choose her own path and negotiate, if need be, with emperors, kings, ambassadors, and congressmen for what she wanted.

She grew quickly adept at reading the motives of her enemies and allies alike, and she now clearly understood that men with power operated in their own best interest. She would do the same. She knew what she wanted: to secure a future for her son and to find a way out of Baltimore. The question was, How to achieve both?

In 1807 Bo, as the three-year-old Jerome Napoleon Bonaparte was called, was a handsome, healthy child with an uncertain legal and social status. In Europe he was the illegitimate son of the king of Westphalia. In America he was the sole offspring of a marriage still recognized as legal in Maryland. He was the grandson of one of America's wealthiest citizens and the natural nephew of the emperor of France. Above all, he carried the surname Bonaparte, and this alone made him an object of considerable interest on both continents. Perhaps most significant, he would become a pawn in a struggle between William Patterson and Elizabeth Patterson Bonaparte, for each believed his choice of loyalty would vindicate their respective actions.

Betsy might have pursued a course of action that reduced, if not resolved, the importance of her son's paternity. She could have quickly filed for a divorce in her home state and just as quickly remarried, giving Bo a father figure and a refuge from political intrigue and social notoriety. This was a choice William Patterson would surely have approved. It was true that Betsy was not a widow, the most respectable status for remarriage; but a dowry from her father could have swept away any concerns about this. Her family wealth, her beauty, and what many saw as her tragic betrayal combined to make her desirable to several eligible bachelors. But Betsy had no intention of remarrying. She meant instead to fight for recognition of her son as a full member of the French imperial family. She meant to see him ranked among the successors to the throne of France. She had once thrown down a challenge to Napoleon— "Tell him that Madame Bonaparte is ambitious and demands her rights as a member of the imperial family." Now it was Bo's rights that consumed her thoughts and that would shape many of her actions for the rest of her life. It seemed not to occur to her, until it was too late, that Bo did not value those "rights" as much as his mother did.

Betsy's attention was no longer focused on her former husband, the king of Westphalia. She dismissed him, and his excuses for abandoning her, with contempt. In November 1807, when an American visitor to Jérôme's court wrote to Betsy that the king "speaks of you as the only woman he ever loved or ever shall love tho' united to another much against his Inclination which the Emperor his Brother cruelly imposed on him," Betsy was unimpressed. On the margin of the letter, she later wrote her own commentary: "The Kindness of my ExHusband the King was ever of the unremitting kind as no money accompanied it."

It was Napoleon, not Jérôme, who she believed could provide Bo with the recognition she desired so intensely for him. And there were many who believed the emperor would do just that. Eliza Anderson, who had accompanied Betsy on the *Erin,* wrote to her at the end of May 1808 with news she had received from France. The emperor, Eliza declared, intended to make Betsy duchess regent of someplace or another. The news was little more than rumor, Eliza admitted, but she was convinced it reflected Napoleon's softened attitude toward the woman he had once dismissed as "that little girl." "It is a sign that you are thought of," Eliza noted, "which gives some hope." A few days later Eliza sent a second letter from her home in Trenton, New Jersey. After telling Betsy that everyone admires the "dignity which I tell them characterizes you in your present Situation," she assured her friend that "a brilliant destiny awaits you and the dear little Bo." On June 8 she wrote once more, promising Betsy that Bo would be "splendidly provided for" and that his mother would surely receive generous support from Napoleon.

Betsy had no intention of sitting back and waiting for the

good fortune that Eliza was confident would come her way. On July 9 she wrote to the current French minister to the United States asking for his assistance in communicating to Napoleon about his nephew. She was careful to place no blame on the emperor; she saw herself, she told General Louis-Marie Turreau, simply as a victim of circumstances outside her control. But if political necessities trumped individual needs or desires, and if the rights of a society superseded the rights of an individual, as they did in her case, surely Napoleon must see Bo in a different light. Bo was no ordinary individual like herself; Bonaparte blood ran in his veins, and thus he was "worthy of interest." As Bo's mother, she found Napoleon's insistence that she call herself Miss Patterson rather than Madame Bonaparte a social embarrassment for them both.

Minister Turreau did not dismiss her appeal out of hand. Instead, he sent her a series of questions meant to test her willingness to bow to any conditions Napoleon might impose. Although these questions were, on the surface, personal, it was clear that Napoleon's motives were political. He wished to prevent any further diplomatic advantage to his archenemy, Britain. His goal was to neutralize this troublesome woman, to ensure that her "plight" would never again be grist for the English propaganda mill. Would she, the emperor's surrogate asked, promise never to marry without the consent of the French government if the emperor gave her a title and a pension? Would she renounce forever any idea of going to England? Would she renounce the United States and go to Europe? If she moved to Europe, would she consent not to leave the town chosen by the emperor for her residence without first informing the prefect of the place? If Betsy agreed to these restrictions, she would, in effect, cede control over where and with whom she lived to Napoleon. This she seemed willing to do. But the last question gave her pause: Do you demand that your son should remain with you until the age of seven? This was itself a demand that she turn over her son at that point, to Napoleon or someone of his choosing.

By September it was clear that her former husband, Jérôme, might be the "someone" who planned to take Bo away. That month Alexandre Le Camus arrived in New York and forwarded to Betsy two letters written in May by Jérôme, one addressed to her and one to William Patterson. Addressing her once again as "beloved Elisa," he asked that she give up her son to him. "Do not give in to grief, my good Elisa," he added, "be hopeful, and count on a happier future." He failed, of course, to provide details of what this happier future might be for a mother who sacrificed her son. In his letter to William, Jérôme was blunt: he wanted to bring up his son in Westphalia and, he claimed, Napoleon had approved of the plan.

Jérôme's conciliatory tone vanished in his next letter. Perhaps he had gotten wind of Betsy's negotiations with Turreau; perhaps he had simply heard rumors that she was attempting to communicate directly with his older brother. Whether it was gossip or fact, Jérôme was offended by the possibility that she would not rely exclusively upon him for assistance. I am a king, he reminded her, and I can provide for you and our son. He clearly thought he was making a magnanimous gesture when

he told Betsy that she could come to Westphalia and keep Bo
with her until the boy turned twelve. He promised more. He
would make her the princess of Smalkalden, a small town that
lay thirty leagues from the capital city, Cassel, and provide her
with a beautiful home and 200,000 francs a year.

Betsy's reply is lost, but at some point she wrote comments on
the margins of his letter. She owed him nothing, she observed,
and the only rights he had over her were the "right to be
despised and hated." She dismissed the offer of a title as princess
of Smalkalden, writing, "Westphalia [is] not large enough for
two queens." But her contempt for Jérôme came through most
clearly when she contemplated choosing between Napoleon's
assistance and Jérôme's: "I would rather be sheltered under the
wings of an eagle than dangle from the beak of a goose."

It may have been satisfying to vent her anger and show her
contempt for this "goose," but Betsy's first consideration was,
after all, Bo's future. What if Jérôme's new wife had no sons?
Would Bo then be heir to his father's throne? Was she indeed
being selfish? Was she letting her feelings toward Jérôme cloud
her judgment? She did not know. She decided to write to the
former ambassador to France, James Monroe, for advice.

Despite Jérôme's assurances, she told Monroe in October
1808 that she worried that Bo might in reality "be consigned to
obscurity by being probably educated in an inferior condition
& in ignorance of his birth & name." She was ready to sacrifice
herself for her son: "My maternal duties certainly prescribe a
total dereliction of all self interested motives & I possess sufficient energy to submit implicitly to any privation how painful

soever which the interest of my son dictate." But, Betsy asked, were Jérôme's promises real? She did not need to remind James Monroe, or herself, how empty Jérôme's promises to her had proven to be.

Monroe replied in early November. He knew the "hard destiny which has attended you" and admired her response to it. She had behaved perfectly and with great dignity. In his judgment, Napoleon was smart enough to realize that, if anything bad happened to Bo in Westphalia, it would be a stain on his own reputation. The real danger, he thought, would come from Queen Catherine, especially if she produced a family. To Monroe, the matter boiled down to this: Would Bo be better off with his father or in the circle of his maternal relatives?

The following spring Betsy reached out to General John Armstrong, the current American minister at Paris. By this time, negotiations with "the eagle," Napoleon, had been going on for almost a year, and Betsy knew that a "necessary provision" for herself was now on the table. She did not want Armstrong to carry on the negotiations without consulting her first. She would not agree to Bo going to France without her. But she was flexible as to the terms of her own settlement. She was resolved, she said, "to accede to any offer which guarantees to me an independent & respectable Situation in life. . . . Should I be offered a title & Pension I will certainly accept them. I prefer infinitely a residence in France to one here." In short, Napoleon's largesse could satisfy her most urgent personal goal: escape from Baltimore.

Betsy's expectations and demands appeared likely to be met.

Napoleon, busy campaigning in Spain, had nevertheless taken the time to comment on the matter in November 1808, although Turreau did not receive his instructions until the spring of 1809. The emperor seemed willing to give Betsy everything she desired—and more. "Tell Turreau that he is to inform her that I will receive with pleasure her son and will be responsible for him if she wishes to send him to France; as for her, whatever she may desire will be granted; that she may count on my esteem and my wish to be agreeable to her; that, when I refused to recognize her, I was led by considerations of high policy; that I am resolved to assure for her son a future that she desires." All Napoleon demanded was that the affair "be quietly and secretly managed."

If "high policy" had motivated Napoleon's annulment of Betsy's marriage, it may have played an equally important role in the olive branch he now held out to Betsy. For the physical desire she had once aroused in Jérôme was now raging in two current suitors. And now as then, the courtship of the belle of Baltimore had political implications, for both of the men hoping to marry her were English.

Chapter Six

"I Intend to Be Governed by My Own Rules"

Betsy had once enjoyed celebrity in America as the happy young bride of a Bonaparte. Now, the tragic tale of her abandonment and persecution at the hands of the Bonapartes drew public attention. The romance of her tragedy worked like an aphrodisiac on young men, and soon after she arrived home, suitors appeared at her doorstep. Although Betsy's full attention was focused on her negotiations with Napoleon, she could not prevent these men from focusing their attention on her.

Her beauty seemed to dazzle those who met her. The English ambassador considered her the "most beautiful woman in America," and when she spent a few months in the nation's capital, anonymous love notes were passed under her hotel door. Even men of the cloth fell under her spell. Reverend Horace Holley, on his way from Boston to Kentucky to take up the duties of a college president, admitted to walking up and down the main street of Baltimore, hoping to meet her. Nothing, not even her vocal hostility toward American culture, could prevent him from confessing to his wife, only half in jest, that in Betsy she had a rival for his affections.

Perhaps if Betsy's most serious admirers had been local Baltimore merchants or Washington officeholders, their pursuit of her affections would only have prompted admiration or envious gossip. But two of her most persistent suitors, Samuel Graves and Charles Oakley, were highly placed Englishmen, and this made their success or failure a source of political anxiety and rumination.

Such entanglement of romance and politics was not new in Betsy's life, of course. Only a few years earlier her marriage to a Frenchman, and a Bonaparte at that, had spurred political speculation about a possible shift from neutrality to a pro-French policy on the part of the American president. Now that she had returned to America, a new set of questions arose: What were the international implications of a marriage between Betsy and one of her two prominent English suitors? Would the transfer of her affections from a French husband to an English one enrage the French? How would the British react? How would American voters respond to Betsy's marriage to an Englishman? Betsy's personal life once again seemed fraught with political implication, but this time her only thought was how to turn this to her own advantage.

Although Betsy had done nothing to encourage him, Samuel Colleton Graves was undoubtedly in love with her. The twenty-year-old had traveled to America as a secretary to his father, Admiral Graves of the Royal Navy. Here he had caught sight of the beautiful Madame Bonaparte—and fallen immediately in love. On May 16, 1808, he confessed his devotion in a letter marked by an odd combination of boldness and insecurity, not to mention tortured sentence structure. "When I first saw you," Graves gushed, your beauty won my admiration, & since that you have acquired most truly (to call it no other) my esteem & my regard, I regretted that seclusion and dereliction should be the lot of youth and beauty, and determined to require your hand in marriage, if your opinion do not operate against me, or your situation when explained, appear to be such as to preclude an object so strongly desired by me. In this preliminary I make only a simple proposition, to entertain an idea that it will offend you, would much afflict me, but I write with confidence, when I say I am sure that at least politeness, will bid you favor me with an answer, if that answer is by return of post it will much oblige me, the tenor if this letter sufficiently indicates that anything like insult, that anything like offence to you, is most remote to the wishes of your devoted S Colleton Graves.

In short, Graves was ready to marry her immediately but would settle for her willingness to begin a courtship.

Betsy might have found Samuel's adoration flattering, but she showed no signs that his passion was—or would ever be—returned. She had no interest in marrying him, or anyone, especially in 1808, when her only concern was securing her son's "brilliant destiny" and achieving a successful escape from her father's household. She had no intention of repeating past mistakes; she would not rely on a callow youth to rescue her. Napoleon, not the young Mr. Graves, held her future in his hands. Yet she sympathized with her suitor, for she knew what it was like to be young and madly in love. Because of this she made every effort to avoid crushing the spirit of her overzealous suitor.

Graves proved persistent if not perceptive. A year after his

opening salvo, he was writing to her once again from Philadelphia. He was, he said, headed home to England but intended
to return to America as soon as possible to press his suit once
again. "In returning," he wrote, "I have but one object, that one
is but too powerful."

Two days later Betsy sent a letter addressed to Samuel and
included with it a note to his father, the admiral. She clearly
intended the older man to read what she had to say to his son.
Her rejection was put as tactfully but as firmly as possible: "I
should extremely regret that a sentiment more painful to yourself should impel a voyage, the result of which can only be disappointment. My time & attachment must be devoted exclusively
to my Son from whose destiny whether inauspicious or the
reverse I can never divide myself. The resolution of consecrat-
ing to him every sentiment & action of my life, is irrevocable—
which with other Circumstances peculiar to myself, will ever
preclude a change of my Situation."

The admiral should have recognized that Samuel had been
politely rejected. But affection for his son, who was clearly in
agony, prompted him to support a second effort to change
Betsy's mind. On July 27, 1809, the younger Graves wrote to
her once again from England. "After the letter I received from
you last May . . . I should not have again addressed you, were
not my affection stronger than my hope." Despite all efforts
to forget her, "the warmth of my attachment is unchilled by
absence, is unabated by time and distance." Because of this, he
confessed, he had enlisted his parents in the effort to change her
mind. "The enclosed," he declared, "is the expression of their

sentiments." And indeed, enclosed with his own declaration that his "love will be as lasting as my recollection" were letters from his mother and father.

Mrs. Graves addressed Betsy as one mother to another: your maternal devotion is admirable, she wrote, but surely your son would be better off with his paternal relatives; why not turn him over to the Bonapartes and thus free yourself to marry my son? The advice regarding Bo's future was both unwelcome and presumptuous, and what followed it was a burst of English patriotism. If Betsy would consent to marry Samuel, Mrs. Graves declared, "My husband & myself will accompany our Son to meet you at Paris to celebrate Nuptials." There was, of course, no possibility of Betsy entering Europe, let alone marrying an Englishman in the capital of France, as long as Napoleon remained emperor. And in 1809 Mrs. Graves's assumption of a speedy victory by Britain in its efforts to unseat the French emperor might well be seen as folly.

Betsy felt compelled to reply: on December 1, 1809, she wrote to Mrs. Graves. She had no intention of turning Bo over to the Bonapartes, she said, and no intention of marrying Samuel. Once again she phrased her rejection as gently but firmly as possible, assuring Samuel's doting if impolitic mother that her son was thoroughly admirable. "I feel regret at having inspired an attachment in Mr. Graves to whose superiority of talent & acquirements I render justice."

Betsy's rejection transformed Samuel's eager optimism into melancholy. He fled to Germany in an effort, once more, to forget her, he said in July 1810, but alas, he feared he could not. His lovelorn condition persisted for at least one more year, but his heart proved resilient. When he died suddenly in 1823, the thirty-five-year-old Graves would leave an "affectionate and devoted wife" and an infant child.

While Samuel Graves was not a member of the royal family, his father held high rank in the Royal Navy. Thus a marriage between the young man and Betsy might have created some embarrassment for the American government. Napoleon might read it as an American shift away from the policy of neutrality, just as Anthony Merry had done in 1803, when Jefferson entertained Jérôme and Betsy in Washington. Public opinion might have opposed such a marriage as well, for anti-British feelings were running high in 1808 because of the *Chesapeake* affair.

Only a year before, in June 1807, British naval officers from the HMS *Leopard* had boarded the USS *Chesapeake* and demanded that the American commander deliver to them four of his sailors, believed to be British subjects. When the commander refused, the British officers returned to their ship, and immediately afterward the *Leopard*'s guns fired on the American vessel. The *Chesapeake* was forced to surrender. Insult was added to injury when the British commander refused to honor the code of battle between two sovereign nations and rejected the American ship as a prize of war; instead he took the four alleged British subjects and sailed away. This slap in the face to American pride stirred anti-British feelings. On the other hand, rage had been building among American shippers as President Jefferson's 1807 Embargo Act began to cripple the shipping industry. The ban on trade with the two central protagonists,

Britain and France, had already driven former Jeffersonian supporters like William Patterson into the opposition camp. With
tensions running high, it was not unreasonable to worry that
any incident, even the marriage of a Baltimore matron, might
add to the diplomatic crisis that was clearly brewing.

These concerns proved even greater when rumors spread that
Sir Charles Oakley had emerged as Betsy's other serious suitor.
Local gossips in Baltimore were betting that Oakley, secretary
to the British ambassador in America, would be the man to win
her hand. "Madame Bonaparte makes our streets quite gay,"
observed one local resident. "Oakley the secretary of the legation to his British Majesty is devoted to her, every evening that
he is here, and, he is very little at Washington, he takes tea and
is with her until ten at night. Bets are made whether he will
offer; if so, whether she will accept or decline." Although Betsy
left no record of her feelings about Oakley, it was obvious to this
observer at least that Betsy was interested: "Betsy is dressed with
care every visit he pays, and will make a conquest if she can,
how far beyond, no one knows."

Local gossips were not the only ones keeping a close eye on
Betsy's romantic opportunities. The British ambassador, trying
to stave off war with America following the *Chesapeake* incident, was beside himself over Oakley's lovesick behavior. Try
as he might, he could not get Oakley to leave her side and fulfill his duty to carry critical correspondence back to England.
The ambassador commented in ungentlemanly fashion that
his stubborn underling was "desperately in love . . . with the
cast-off wife of Jerome Bonaparte" and would not set sail for

home until Betsy made up her mind. The French ambassador was equally disturbed. The possibility that the mother of Napoleon Bonaparte's nephew might marry an Englishman troubled Louis-Marie Turreau. The emperor, negotiating with Betsy through Turreau, would not be pleased to see the English press gloat once again that their country had rescued a wronged American woman from the fate that the French ruler had cruelly imposed upon her.

Was Betsy using the threat of a marriage to Oakley as a wedge in her negotiations with Napoleon? The thought might have occurred to Turreau, for a woman who diplomatically signed her letter to the emperor "Eliza nee Patterson" was clearly not naïve. But Betsy knew that the rumor of a possible marriage to Oakley was a double-edged sword: it might prompt Napoleon to act more quickly and to be more generous, but it might just as well provoke him to cut off all negotiations, abandon her son, and deny her the funds she needed to escape Baltimore. In the end, she decided to place her faith in the emperor rather than raise the stakes of the game with him. She made clear to a number of her correspondents in Washington and Paris that she had no intention of marrying Oakley—or any Englishman.

Hearing this news, Turreau breathed a sigh of relief. Although he had not yet learned the final terms of the arrangement made by Napoleon, he agreed to Betsy's request that he advance her the first installment of her expected pension. He provided a credit of $20,000 for her and later arranged for her to receive 60,000 francs a year in monthly installments of $500. He then assigned Louis Tousard to double duty as Betsy's assistant and as his spy on her behavior. Because of the highly charged political atmosphere in 1810, Tousard was also expected to protect Bo from a possible kidnapping attempt by the British or by British sympathizers.

Betsy had played her cards well. But she had also established a pattern that she would not and perhaps could not break: men might court her, but she would not allow herself to be won. She intended, as she would later tell Turreau's successor, "to be governed by my own rules" rather than the rules of any man. Her friend Eliza Anderson observed with dismay the implications of Betsy's vow of independence: "I wonder how many more poor Knights are doomed to beat their hapless wings in thy fine spun web . . . after having led the poor Devils a dance of delirium, they cool off to friendship & commiserate you as a victim of fate." Over the next few years, many men would do the "dance of delirium," from the stolid John Willink of Holland to the grandson of Light Horse Harry Lee. But none would ever persuade Betsy Patterson Bonaparte to turn her fate over to a man again.

Chapter Seven

"I Shall Resume the Name of My Own Family"

Napoleon had actually made no final decision about a settlement with Betsy—and in fact he never would. Yet each month she received 5,000 francs from Turreau. A younger Betsy might have spent this pension on clothes, on the hats she adored, and on many indulgences of the kind she had clearly enjoyed in the days when Jérôme had satisfied every whim that money—or credit—could buy.

But the twenty-four-year-old Betsy was no longer the self-indulgent girl she had once been. Although temptations abounded, she did not buy the "French gloves Fashions &&" that filled Baltimore shops despite the war in Europe. She was willing, however, to make such indulgences easier for friends like Dolley Madison, now the president's wife. Writing to Dolley in November 1813, Betsy offered to shop for her and deliver the requested items on the next trip to Washington. But for herself, she would be satisfied to update old clothing as best she could.

Betsy's parsimony had purpose. Just as her father had done in his earliest years in America, she was scrimping and saving in order to invest. And she proved to have that same keen business sense that had made William a wealthy man. She invested part of each month's pension payment in stocks, accepting small yields in exchange for the security of shares in banks, turnpikes, and established companies. When she accumulated the necessary cash, she began the investment in real estate that would add to her wealth in the future, buying a small house and a lot in downtown Baltimore.

Where once her life had been flamboyant, Betsy now took care to avoid the gossip that came to those in the limelight. After the Oakley rumors, she was determined not to stir any new rumors about her love life. Writing to a friend in 1812, she was careful to declare, "No novelties here, political or amatory." This did not mean, of course, that men had ceased to flock around her. Poetry—most of it bad—poured in from lovesick suitors, and she seemed to have won the hearts of both Henry Lee Jr., the grandson of Light Horse Harry, and John Willink, scion of a prominent Dutch banking family. But Betsy, when she was in Washington, D.C., chose to attend social events on the arm of the seventy-six-year-old vice president, Elbridge Gerry, whose invalid wife, Ann, remained at home in Massachusetts. Gerry sang Betsy's praises to his wife. "The more I see of this lady," he wrote, "the more I like her, and so would all our family. She is amiable, unaffected, unassuming, sensible, and altogether free from a disposition to censure."

Despite her best efforts, however, Betsy's personal history continued to entangle her in politics at home and diplomacy abroad. For it was well known that she was receiving a pension from France, and there were continuing rumors that Napoleon planned to make her a duchess. This might have been acceptable in more stable political moments, but with France and Britain each trying to strangle the trade of the other, American neutrality in the European conflict seemed more fragile than

ever. Britain's continued practice of boarding American ships
and impressing American seamen into service in the Royal
Navy was a blow to national pride, while Napoleon's Berlin and
Milan decrees of 1806 and 1807 increased the threat to American trade with Britain. When Napoleon put his brother Joseph
on the Spanish throne in 1808, making the Spanish colonies
in the Americas loyal to the emperor, members of both parties
began to suspect that Napoleonic ambitions might be a threat
to national security. As America reeled back and forth between
pro- and anti-French and -British sentiments, a general ani-
mosity toward both sides in this European struggle seemed to
emerge. With it came a sharp suspicion of anyone who appeared
too eager to accept favors from Britain or France. No one fit the
description better than Betsy Bonaparte—and she knew it.

It was only a matter of time before a politician took advantage of this new public sentiment. In 1810, during the second
session of the Eleventh Congress, Senator Philip Reed of Betsy's
home state of Maryland proposed an amendment to Article 1,
Section 9, of the Constitution. The original article forbade U.S.
officeholders from receiving "any present, Emolument, Office,
or title, of any kind whatever, from any King, Prince, or foreign state" without the consent of Congress. Reed's proposed
amendment would extend this prohibition to "any citizen of the
United States" and would add, as a penalty, the loss of American
citizenship.

With surprising speed and consensus, Congress approved
Reed's amendment, the Senate voting 19–5 in favor and the
House, 87–3. Federalists, who were always ready to criticize
France and American Francophiles, had thrown their sup-

port behind Reed, despite the fact that he was a Republican. Massachusetts senator Timothy Pickering, an ardent Federalist, insisted that the amendment was necessary to prevent a diabolical plan by Napoleon to establish on American soil "a Court, which in splendor, [would] outshine, & in expences [*sic*] & attentions, surpass, the palace of the first magistrate of our nation." Elizabeth Patterson Bonaparte and her son, declared Pickering, were the core around which this decadence that would erode the republic would be formed. For his part, Pickering thought it would be wise to ban anyone with royal blood from living in the United States.

By the end of 1811, ten states had ratified the "titles of nobility" amendment, and two more ratified in 1812. Had it won the three remaining states, Betsy would have faced a difficult if not impossible decision: Should she renounce her French pension and abandon all hopes of obtaining French aid for her son, or should she continue to receive payments from a foreign state and risk losing her citizenship? Friends and lawyers suggested that she try to renegotiate the terms of her pension, either by asking for a lump-sum payment that would cover Bo's educational expenses or by channeling all the pension payments into a trust for Bo. But Betsy saw the danger in asking for any change in the mode of payment. The amendment might hurt her, she conceded, but entering into new negotiations with the French might have equally dire consequences. Instead, she hastened to assure the French legation that she had not and would not seek any change in the arrangements they had made. Fortunately, the titles of nobility amendment fell short of adoption, and when the War of 1812 established Britain as the nation's enemy,

public concern about Betsy Patterson Bonaparte's French connections faded.

If the danger from the government at home was over for
Betsy, she still faced problems from abroad. For in the very
year that the United States went to war with Britain, Jérôme
Bonaparte decided to write once again to the woman whom he
persisted in calling his American wife. It had been three years
since Betsy had heard from the man who was now king of Westphalia, but the letter had a familiar ring to it. Jérôme insisted
that he remained her true and loving friend and that he had
her best interests at heart. He urged her to be patient, and he
would provide for her. Two months after she received this letter,
Betsy's brother Joseph encountered Jérôme in Paris. After being
reassured that Betsy had not married an Englishman, Jérôme
pledged to take immediate steps to see Napoleon bring Betsy
and Bo safely to France. The next morning, however, Joseph
learned that Jérôme had left town. He did not contact Joseph
again. If her brother was surprised by this turn of events, Betsy
surely was not. The "bill of a goose" might clack and quack, but
it would never provide her shelter.

Betsy found it easy to ignore Jérôme's empty promises. But
she could not ignore the precarious legal position she remained
in as long as, under Maryland law, he was still her husband.
For according to marital law here and in all American states, a
husband was entitled to control the finances of his wife. A single
woman, however, could control her own wealth, make her own
investments, and devise her own will. This was reason enough
for Betsy to file for divorce. In 1812 she did just that, and the

Maryland legislature granted her request. On December 15, 1812, "an act annulling the marriage of Jérôme Bonaparte, and Elizabeth Bonaparte of the city of Baltimore" declared the marriage null and void. Nothing in the act, however, was to be construed to make Bo's birth illegitimate. The assembly's ruling, combined with the French legislation demanded by Napoleon in 1805, made Betsy legally free of Jérôme on both the European and the American continents. Her growing fortune was entirely her own.

Less than four months after Betsy's divorce decree, Napoleon's world collapsed. On April 6, 1813, the emperor of France was forced to abdicate his throne and was sent into exile on the island of Elba. Some in America rejoiced at this news, even if it meant Britain's military and naval attention could now be turned to its American war. Perhaps Betsy should have been one of them. But she did not celebrate the downfall of Napoleon Bonaparte. All her life she remained an admirer of the man who annulled her marriage, refused to allow her to set foot on the European continent, and "hurled me back on what I hated most on earth, my Baltimore obscurity." She spoke frankly of her admiration for the fallen emperor. She respected his ambition, his self-confidence, the power of his personality, and, above all, the fact that he had for so long been master of his own destiny. It was ironic that the only man in Betsy's life who shared these character traits was William Patterson, the domineering, proud, self-made man with whom she could never make her peace.

Napoleon's fall shook Europe, and it shook Betsy's world as well. She realized with finality that she would not be made a duchess; she would not be given a palace of her own. Bo would not, as rumor had so often insisted, be made a grand duke. And the pension she had received for almost six years would soon dry up. Fortunately for Betsy, the wheels of bureaucracy turned slowly in the nineteenth century, and she continued to receive her monthly payment for six more months while the French government adjusted to life without Napoleon Bonaparte.

In one important way, Napoleon's downfall was cause for celebration for Betsy: the ban on her travel to Europe was lifted. As she told Dolley Madison on December 29, 1814, "The obstacles which the Emperor Napoleon opposed to my continual desire of residing in Paris, have ceased with his Power." She was now, she continued with obvious relief, convinced of her "unimportance with the actual French Government," so much so that she believed it was unnecessary to even consult with them about her coming to their country. Her more "timid friends," however, were less convinced that she could enter France without incident, and so she had asked Victor Louis Charles, the Duc de Caraman, to make inquiries for her. The result was reassuring. "I have ascertained beyond all doubt," Betsy wrote, "what I before supposed, that I shall enjoy in Europe exactly the same privileges with any other American Lady who finds it agreeable to travel there." To further ensure that she would be seen as just another American tourist, she would enter France not as Elizabeth Bonaparte but as Elizabeth Patterson. "On leaving this Country, I shall resume the name of my own Family & abandon one which produced me so much unhappiness." Her only problem was finding respectable traveling companions, for as a single woman, it was unseemly for her to make the transatlantic voyage alone. She asked Dolley to use her influence to persuade an American couple headed to Holland to allow her to accompany them.

Despite all her efforts, these plans fell through. The war with Britain was at her doorstep, and the Patterson family was in disarray. The British had set up a blockade of American ports, making any voyage dangerous. And after taking Washington in August 1814, a British army headed toward Baltimore that September. With Fort McHenry under attack, no passenger ship was likely to sail.

Even had the war not come to Betsy's hometown, family pressures would have delayed her departure. In January 1814, Betsy's younger sister, Caroline, wrote to her in Washington that their mother "was very sick but better now." Sometime over the next few months, however, Dorcas Spear Patterson's condition worsened. On May 21, 1814, at the age of fifty-two, she died. Mother and daughter had always been close, and Betsy felt the loss deeply. Whether William Patterson mourned the loss of his wife is unknown; as Betsy would frequently bitterly note, he had enjoyed a fairly steady stream of mistresses while her mother was alive, fathering a daughter with one of these women. Even as his wife lay ill and dying, William had been callous enough to bring one of these women to live in the family home.

In truth, the loss of his wife seemed to trouble William far less that the contraction of the household he reigned over. In 1808 his son and namesake had died; his daughter Margaret, only seventeen, had passed away in 1811; and twelve-year-old Octavius soon followed. Marriage had taken others away: Robert Patterson had married his sweetheart, Marianne Caton, and moved out of the family home. John, also married, now lived in Virginia. Joseph was in Europe, and Edward had virtually moved into the Smith home, as he was about to marry one of Sam's daughters. Where once William had been the master of a household filled with children, only nineteen-year-old George and fourteen-year-old Henry remained. Far worse than the absence of sons and daughters was the fact that, with Dorcas's death, the Patterson household was without a woman to oversee its domestic operations—and see to its patriarch's needs.

It soon became clear that William expected his daughter Betsy to fill the position left empty by Dorcas's death. Although Napoleon's abortive effort to reclaim power failed in 1815 and peace finally came to Europe, and although the British blockade was lifted, William pressured Betsy to remain in Baltimore.

In early-nineteenth-century American society, bowing to a father's wishes was more common than defying them. And in any respectable, genteel American family, unmarried women were expected to remain at home rather than take themselves off to foreign countries on their own. Respectable mothers did not abandon their children, even if they left them in the good hands of relatives or friends. Yet Betsy proved willing to break all these rules. Learning of Betsy's decision to go abroad, one of her neighbors remarked: "This scheme requires a decided character to go through with it." Elizabeth Patterson Bonaparte had just the character that was needed. On July 26, 1815, she arrived in Liverpool. She was thirty years old—and this was the first trip she had ever taken alone. It would not be her last.

Betsy's father, William Patterson, in his early thirties, by noted English artist
Robert Edge Pine. Posed as a prosperous young merchant,
Patterson joined General Horatio Gates, George II, and Maryland's
Charles Carroll as one of Pine's elite subjects.
(Courtesy of the Maryland Historical Society)

In 1806 Gilbert Stuart painted three aspects of the beautiful young
Elizabeth Patterson Bonaparte. Fifty years later, George D'Almaine
created this pastel copy of Stuart's famous portrait.
(Courtesy of the Maryland Historical Society)

Girolamo Buonaparte, born on
the island of Corsica, later known
as Jérôme Bonaparte, was the
youngest brother of Napoleon I.
This watercolor portrait of Jérôme
in his naval uniform, painted by
Francesco Emanuele Scotto, was
probably completed in 1806, when
Jérôme was twenty-one years old.
*(Courtesy of the Maryland
Historical Society)*

Edward Patterson, brother of Betsy, painted by the self-taught artist William Edward West around 1839. Edward, born in 1789, was Betsy's confidant and favorite sibling. Although a talented pianist, Edward gave up any musical ambition to join his father's shipping business.
(Courtesy of the Maryland Historical Society)

Pauline Bonaparte, the Princess Borghese, the sister of Napoleon I and Jérôme Bonaparte, reputed to be the most beautiful woman in Europe as well as one of the most libertine. Born in 1780, she died in Rome at the age of forty-four of pulmonary tuberculosis.
(Photograph: Walter Marc. © RMN-Grand Palais/Art Resource, NY. Chateaux de Malmaison et Bois-Preau, Rueil-Malmaison, France)

Around 1817, Flemish painter and miniaturist François Kinsoen completed this oil painting of the thirty-two-year-old Betsy Bonaparte. Between 1808 and 1813, Kinsoen had been the official court painter for Betsy's former husband, Jérôme, King of Westphalia.
(Courtesy of the Maryland Historical Society)

Jérôme Bonaparte at sixteen years old and beginning his career as an officer in the French navy. Oil portrait.
(Courtesy of the Maryland Historical Society)

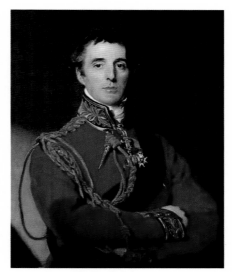

Arthur Wellesley, first Duke of Wellington, was forty-five years old when Sir Thomas Lawrence painted this portrait in 1814, only a few months before the Battle of Waterloo. *(Wellington Museum, London)*

Jerome Napoleon Bonaparte in his midforties. Daguerreotype, photographer unknown. "Bo" was born in England and grew up in Baltimore, where he lived until his death in 1870. In 1829 he married the heiress Susan May Williams. Their two sons, Jerome (known as Junior) and Charles, were Betsy's only grandchildren. *(Courtesy of the Maryland Historical Society)*

Jerome Napoleon Bonaparte, Jr., older son of Betsy's only child,
"Bo," was around twenty when he sat for this portrait. He graduated
from West Point Academy in 1852 but resigned his commission
in 1854 and went on to serve with distinction in the army
of his cousin, Napoleon III of France. *(Courtesy of the
Maryland Historical Society)*

Charles Joseph Bonaparte and
his wife, Ellen Channing
Day Bonaparte
*(Courtesy of the Maryland
Historical Society)*

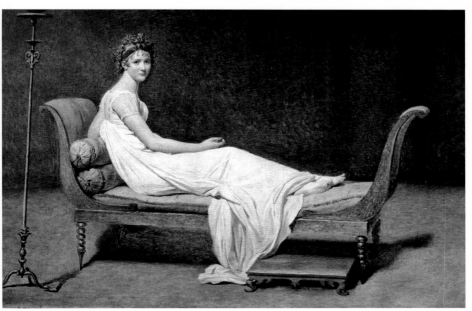

Jeanne-Françoise Julie Adélaïde Récamier was twenty-three when she sat
for this uncompleted portrait by Jacques-Louis David in 1800. *(The Louvre)*

Jérôme Bonaparte.
Portrait by Sophie Lienard.

Chapter Eight

"The Purposes of Life Are All Fulfilled"

When Betsy set sail for England, she left behind a furious father, a saddened son, and a collection of disappointed suitors. William's insistence that she do her familial duty had fallen on deaf ears. Her young son's tears had not shaken her resolve. And the lovesick poems of her most ardent suitor that year, William Johnson Jr., had not given her pause. Johnson's pleas—"O Turn thou lovely Eyes away / I cannot bear the melting Ray"—and his pleading letters—"What if I am not able to drive you from my thoughts? Or even my Dreams?"—so like those of Samuel Graves, could not persuade Betsy that her future lay in America as the proper wife of a solid citizen.

Betsy had prepared for her trip as carefully as she could. She had elicited letters of introduction from a number of Washington political figures, local businessmen, and old friends like Thomas Jefferson. Jefferson feared that he could be of little service; he reminded her that it had been twenty-five years since he had been to Paris, and all the important people he had known during his years as ambassador to France had been "swept away" by the violence of the last few decades. But Betsy's uncle, Samuel Smith, provided her with a letter of introduction to the Marquis de Lafayette. Richard Gilmore sent notes to friends in the Netherlands, including the wife of the Dutch bureaucrat who had permitted the *Erin* to be restocked in 1803, introducing Betsy as an amiable woman with an "interesting history." And Jan Willink, father of another of Betsy's disappointed suitors, wrote to his brother William, urging him to assist Betsy in any way she requested.

William Patterson had also been busy writing friends and business associates in Europe, but his letters would be of no help to his daughter. In them, he portrayed Betsy as a mentally unbalanced young woman who had left home "contrary to the Wishes of her friends." He asked London banker James McIlhiny to monitor her behavior and report her actions to her concerned father. McIlhiny revealed William's request to Betsy, perhaps believing that the call for someone to spy on a daughter was a sign of paternal concern and affection. Betsy thought not. Fifty-two years later she would annotate McIlhiny's letter with a cold fury that matched her father's unkindness: she "conceived a residence under [her father's] Roof," she wrote, "to be the hole of the asp & the den of the Cockatrix." She still keenly felt her need to escape from William's flaunting of mistresses a half century later. But it was her keen feeling of rejection, of holding second place in William's affections, that still burned most brightly. His mistresses, she noted, "were more congenial company to the venerable Pater familias as well a bad Example to his daughter—He was delighted at her departure & had done Every thing in his power to get rid of her."

Yet not even William's cruel characterization of Betsy as mentally unbalanced could diminish her joy at being in England again. That nation, still celebrating its victory over Napoleon, proved more than ready to welcome the woman who exemplified in 1815, as she had in 1803, the callousness of the former emperor. The English were ready to overlook her disregard for those social conventions that prevented a woman, and a mother, from traveling without a male guardian. Members of the nobility and prominent families flooded her with invitations, eager to provide the hospitality that Napoleon had denied her.

Betsy threw herself into the social life they offered. She rented a small cottage in the fashionable spa town of Cheltenham, insisting that her health had been so damaged by the tensions of life in Baltimore that taking the waters at Cheltenham was essential to her recovery. Whether this was true or not, it provided her with a reason to quit the company of the American couple who had chaperoned her on the Atlantic crossing. Soon after she settled in, she could be seen attending rounds of dinner parties and musical concerts with new friends like Sir Arthur and Lady Brooke Falkener. The Falkeners' friendship was invaluable, for as Betsy noted, England was a country "so particular about social position that relations with persons of obscure background, however honorable and respectable they may be, are not tolerated." Safely under the wing of the Falkeners, Betsy could report to her father her many invitations to balls hosted by the nobility. Here as in Washington, Betsy's beauty impressed all who saw her. When she appeared at a ball, dressed in an "embroidered high-waisted muslin dress, ermine-lined cloak, diamond studded tiara in her . . . hair" and wearing an emerald necklace given to her by Jérôme, men hurried to her side. By August she had reached the pinnacle of social acceptance: she received an invitation to a garden party to be held at the pavilion of the Prince of Wales. Here she mingled with Lord Castlereagh and two of the prince's former mistresses, Lady Melbourne and Lady Hertford. All doors seemed open to her now. She was invited to exclusive gambling clubs like Almack's, where she saw Beau Brummel himself, and she whiled away afternoons playing whist and faro at the homes of Lady Archer and Lady Buckingham.

Her delight and her relief at her own success were obvious: three thousand miles from home, she at last felt "cherished, visited, respected, and admired." Betsy took pains to explain the happiness she felt to her father. "Europe more than meets the brilliant and vivid colors in which my imagination portrayed it. Its resources are infinite, much beyond those which can be offered us in a new country. The purposes of life are all fulfilled, activity and repose without monotony. Beauty commands homage, talents secure admiration, misfortune meets with respect."

But William was not impressed by his daughter's social success. His only response to Betsy's accounts of her crowded social calendar was to write: "I am convinced that the happiness you are seeking is not true happiness; I pray to God that you will see your error." Surely his cruelest comment followed. "As for your letters," he told his daughter, "I am so ashamed of them that I do not dare show them to anybody."

William's disapproval hung like a cloud over Betsy. He was, and he would ever remain, the true audience for her social success, and he would forever refuse to admire or respect it. His criticism was echoed in the letters of James McIlhiny, who adopted a paternal tone that was chillingly familiar to Betsy. Like William, McIlhiny disapproved of her independent behavior. He wrote to her from London on September 5, 1815, chiding her for parting company with her chaperones. She was, he said, inviting scandal. "I fear it may give room for ill-natured things to be said of you and you must know the world full well enough to find that the Natural Disposition of Mankind is prone to Evil and Consequently Censorious." He urged her not to go out in public so much and seemed convinced that everyone at home was shocked at her departure from America. As he understood it, she had simply run away, "without any of your Family being apprised of your Intentions." Far worse, even her "poor Dear Boy" had known nothing of her intentions to abandon him.

Betsy did her best to assure McIlhiny that she had neither stolen off in the night nor abandoned her child. She had left him in the capable and affectionate care of her brother Robert and his wife. He was never far from her thoughts, she assured McIlhiny, and she was eager to investigate European schools for Bo. But the rumors that she was a runaway mother persisted, spread, it seemed, by her own relatives. Betsy's brother Edward, one of her few family allies, was appalled when she told him that members of their extended family had criticized her departure. "It was with the most mortifying indignation that I read of the conduct of our relations in London. What could have prompted this behavior is inconceivable had you not recieved [*sic*] your information from an undoubted source I could not but be incredulous." Edward knew the truth and stated it simply: "We all knew you were going."

By November, letters of denial and assertions of innocence came pouring in to Betsy from the offending family members. John Spear Smith wrote from Baltimore that he was certain none of her relatives had expressed the slightest opposition to her trip abroad. A hint of envy at her situation crept into his note as he added that life in Baltimore was "the same old and dull . . . nothing but eating drinking and sleeping indeed since the war we are more flat than ever." Ann Spear's denial was more emphatic. We never said such things, she insisted, but she could not refrain from adding, "I think it both wicked & ridiculous to make such a groaning about it even if it were true." In her view, Betsy was guilty of overreacting. "I am sure," she declared, "if you had lost an eye or a leg you could not have grieved more." And, on December 27, Betsy's cousin Mary Mansfield attempted to dismiss the matter as an unfortunate misunderstanding. She had learned, she said, that Betsy was angry about "tales allegedly spread by me about you."

Betsy knew that the main source of the problem was not her cousins but her own father. Years later, as she annotated the correspondence she had saved for half a century, she wrote on the back of McIlhiny's September 5 letter: "Health Character attention what were they to the insane miser who desired only an excuse to blot all out respecting his Conduct so dastardly to a poor & defenceless woman."

Among Betsy's family correspondents that year, only her brother Edward sent genuine good wishes. "This will find you, I hope enjoying all the fashionable amusements of London—we go on in the same old train, just as dull as ever no public amusements & precious few private ones—what a contrast there must be between London & Baltimore!" What John Spear Smith envied, Edward took vicarious delight in.

For Betsy, the contrast between life at home and life abroad was tangible. While her Baltimore family went on "in the same old train," Betsy dined at the home of the Duke of Wellington, hero of Waterloo. She was introduced to men of talent, like the painter Benjamin West, and to women of noble breeding, like Lady Godfrey Webster. Reveling in her social success, Betsy soon forgave her relatives for their criticisms. But she could not resist writing a sharp rebuke to her father. "It appears to me," she wrote, "that, if I have friends in America, their friendship might have been shown in a more agreeable mode than finding fault with me for being miserable in a country where I never was appreciated, and where I can never be contented."

As this letter reveals, Betsy could not and would never understand why she was criticized simply because she believed life in Europe suited her better than life in America. She was not proselytizing; she made no effort to convert others to her views of the relative value of life abroad and at home. She knew, as she told John Spear Smith months later in August 1816, that Americans "consider me an apostate from the Republic, an impudent & successful imitator of high life, which they profess to despise in short a bad Citizen"; yet Betsy believed she had had no choice but to leave her native country. She asked only that friends and family—and above all, her father—accept what she was certain was true: that she had been born in the wrong place, in a culture that did not suit her interests or talents, and in a world in which she would always feel a misfit and an outsider. Her wit, her intelligence, and her love of cultured life meant that she did not belong in a society of practical, business-oriented men and docile, domestic women whose conversation centered on either money or children and for whom routine was more desirable than novelty of experience. She required a public life that carried with it the chance to mingle with men and women who were her equals in intellect and in the art of social intercourse. In Baltimore, she suffocated; in London and in the capitals of Europe, she was able to breathe at last.

William did not understand the attraction public life held for his daughter. It surely held no charm for him. In his mind, social interactions were necessary only to accomplish other goals; they were never ends in themselves. Nor could he understand the desire of a woman to carve out a place in the public sphere. In a proper society, that sphere was—and ought to be—a masculine domain. An eccentric spinster like Betsy's aunt Nancy Spear, avidly following the debates on the floor of Congress, was bad enough, but his own daughter, traipsing off to Europe alone, abandoning her duties to her child and her father—this was a rejection of woman's essentially submissive nature and her proper destiny that he could neither fathom nor tolerate. He could only conclude that his daughter was a fool, and a willful fool at that. No matter how hard she tried to show that she was "prudent and wise," guilty only of making choices he would not have made, he clung to the notion that her life was a fool's errand. Small wonder that, until death separated them, father and daughter would remain bitterly at odds.

In 1815 William effectively expressed his anger at his daughter by withdrawing financial support for her. This surprised and shocked even James McIlhiny, who told William so. William fired back, saying that it was improper for his daughter to live abroad without the protection of her family. He could only hope that she would "satisf[y] her curiosity" and come home. McIlhiny readily agreed with William that in Europe Betsy was an "unprotected female" and that she ought to go home, but he could not condone William's refusal to send funds. He warned Betsy that her income from her investments was not enough to survive on in London or Paris. If she remained in Europe, she would have to take the drastic step of drawing down her capital.

Unlike McIlhiny, Betsy was not surprised by her father's refusal to send support. But she thought William's decision was based less on her disobedience than on his own flawed character. To her, her father's greatest sin was all too obvious: he abused his patriarchal authority. He had demanded loyalty and devotion from his wife as his due but had shown her little respect in return. And in exchange for paternal protection, he had required that his children always acknowledge that he knew best. Over the years, she believed her father had proven himself a miser and a philanderer, a man without honor. While she was in her darkest moments of disappointment and humiliation, he had thought not of her but of the money he had lost when Jérôme abandoned her. Without hesitation, he had confiscated most of the property and possessions from her marriage. In 1867 her annotation to this letter from McIlhiny wove together seamlessly these two aspects of his selfishness: "Mr Patterson's objection to my residence abroad was an Excuse for never giving me a cent from 1805 to 1835—his Mistress Nancy Todd was in his house when his wife was on her death bed—& when expelled by Edward Patterson was succeeded in the same capacity by Somers by whom he had in old age a bastard daughter."

All Betsy now asked of William was that he stop his public criticism of her behavior. Thinking that perhaps he would be happy if she remarried, she told him his blunt attacks were certain to doom her chances of making a suitable second marriage. "Everyone who knows me has heard that your wealth is enormous, and consequently they think I shall have a large fortune from you. In Europe," she informed him, "a handsome woman who is likely to have a fortune may marry well," but not even a Venus could make a good match if she was poor.

Friends and family in America doubted that either William's parsimony or his criticism could prevent their American Venus from finding a husband. She would turn heads and win hearts in Europe just as she had done in Baltimore. Eliza Anderson, now Eliza Godefroy, wrote to Betsy that March congratulating her on her popularity, especially with the Duke of Wellington, "the Conquerer of Conquerors of the Earth," who Eliza was convinced was "already a victim of your charms."

Betsy was not really interested in finding a husband. More was at stake for her than the loss of that independence that she had embraced so fiercely in Baltimore. It was pride, and her intense concern for her son's future, that made her loath to marry again and thus give up the name Bonaparte. Despite Napoleon's failure to regain his empire, and despite her former husband's less-than-noble character, she believed her son shared an illustrious bloodline. She was convinced that some-day a member of the Bonaparte family would rule France once again, and she did not think it farfetched that Bo might be that man. At the very least, he might join the inner circle of a new Bonaparte empire. As long as this was possible, she was determined to do nothing to cloud his claim to legitimacy with the Bonaparte family. In the meantime, she felt certain that the family name alone would make Bo welcome in the aristocratic society of Europe and ensure his marriage into the nobility. Bo was still just a child, but it was his marital future that concerned Betsy, not her own.

Betsy's most pressing problem was neither husband hunting nor her eleven-year-old son's destiny but her immediate finan-cial straits. She could not really afford to travel in the social circles that welcomed her in England. But the thought of re-turning to Baltimore was unbearable; the mere possibility left her ill and filled her with misery. "In my dreams," she confessed to her sister-in-law, "I am transported to the populous desert of Baltimore and awake shuddering. . . . If I could only know that I should never return to my wretchedness in the United States, I am sure I should get well."

Over the winter and spring, Betsy followed her investments anxiously. In January she received the bad news that the Ameri-can stock market was depressed and the economy stagnant; her insurance stock had produced no dividends. But by May 1816, better news arrived: Betsy's stocks were booming. On May 30 she was relieved to learn that a remittance for 500 pounds sterling was on its way. This transaction had been arranged "with much difficulty" through her father, who demanded the full going rate of 20 percent for his assistance. Although a compromise was reached, Betsy would not forget her father's cold calculations in all his financial exchanges with her. On the back of the letter that detailed the negotiations over the money, Betsy later wrote that her father was "the Plague sore of my life."

By the time she received this much-needed money, Betsy had left England and made her way to Paris. She had received a passport to France and felt that, no matter what the consequences, she could not end her trip without visiting the French capital. She arrived that spring—and took the city by storm.

Chapter Nine

"Your Ideas Soar'd Too High"

All Paris did indeed seem to be at the feet of Elizabeth Patterson Bonaparte. The triumphant Duke of Wellington included her in the many dinner parties and balls he held at the British embassy. And a revitalized French aristocratic society, newly freed from its long suppression by the emperor Napoleon Bonaparte, warmly welcomed the beautiful victim of Bonaparte tyranny. The king himself announced he would like to meet the belle of Baltimore, but Betsy declined his invitation; it was unseemly, she surely felt, to accept the hospitality of her benefactor's successor. Everyone, even those at home who disapproved of Betsy, seemed completely fascinated by her social success. In a letter written in the spring of 1816, John Spear Smith gushed, "It is now generally reported that you set the fashion in Paris! How do you stand the torrent of admiration?"

Most of Betsy's American correspondents focused on the possibility for remarriage that her popularity promised. They could not abandon the conviction that a contented domestic life was every woman's true goal. Her spinster aunt, Nancy Spear, was certain that Betsy had immediately fallen in love—she chided her niece for sending her a Paris dress and shoes that were far too small: "You must certainly be distractedly in love before you could so entirely have forgotten my gigantic shape." It was common knowledge back in Baltimore that Betsy's doors and stairs were thronged with "dukes. Counts. Marquis. Yourself a little Queen—giving and receiving the most supreme happiness," and thus Betsy's friends and relatives were confident that, even without a dowry from William, she would find a suitable husband. "How can you pretend to tell me that there is no love in Europe," one relative wrote, who clearly did not think Betsy's unorthodox past would be a hindrance to finding a man who loved her enough to propose marriage. "Don't we here [sic] every day of English noblemen marrying actresses & that is what we would call love indeed."

It was true that lovesick men pursued Betsy in Paris just as they had in Baltimore, but she found them more annoying and troublesome than appealing. When, for example, the young Chevalier de Saint-Cricq, ten years her junior, declared that should she return home without accepting his proposal, he would follow her to Baltimore, Betsy must have been reminded of her English suitor Samuel Graves. Like Graves's father, Saint-Cricq's father intervened, not to plead his son's case but to beg Betsy to send the young man home should he actually cross the Atlantic in pursuit.

Betsy knew that her beauty and her tragic past had opened many doors wide for her, and she wrote home about her social success in great detail. In August 1816 she recounted to her cousin John Spear Smith that "for some weeks I have been immersed in Balls, Soirees, Dinners which have not left me a single moment." Yet she was also proud that her popularity did not rest alone on her lovely face or her sad history. For Paris was a city with a vibrant intellectual tradition, and it was Elizabeth Patterson Bonaparte's wit and brilliance that brought her many of her most cherished invitations.

Those invitations came from the resurgent salon society of Paris. Now that Napoleon was gone, French intellectuals had returned to the city from their forced or self-imposed exile and had revived the salon life that the emperor had so despised. This renewal of intellectual and artistic life acted as a magnet to poets and novelists from neighboring countries as well. The grandes dames of these salons, where "wit counted for everything," found Betsy worthy of a place at their gatherings.

Betsy was first introduced into this charmed salon circle by one of Albert Gallatin's embassy staff, David Bailie Warden, an Irish revolutionary and American citizen who would remain her good friend over the ensuing years. It was through him that she first met Madame de Staël, the extraordinary woman of letters and champion of women's rights who was as famous for her love affairs with the French political leader Charles-Maurice de Talleyrand and the writer Benjamin Constant as for her essays and her novels. Brilliant and charming, Germaine de Staël was admired by women as much as by men. "If I were a queen," one admirer declared, "I would order Mme De Stael to talk to me always." De Staël had dominated salon culture until the Reign of Terror forced her to flee Paris. She returned briefly in 1794, but Napoleon exiled her the following year. After Waterloo, she, like many other intellectuals, returned to Paris to campaign for liberal causes. She remained a central figure in the city's intellectual community until her death in 1817.

Warden also introduced Betsy to the always hospitable Juliette Récamier, whose charm and beauty attracted men and women of greater intellectual and artistic achievement than her own to her salon. Like De Staël, Madame Récamier had returned from her exile when Napoleon began his. And like Betsy, she would remain sought after by men well into her old age. Perhaps Betsy's closest friend among these remarkable Frenchwomen was Voltaire's adopted daughter, the kindly Reine Philiberte Rouph de Varicourt, Marquise de Villette, who wrote under the sobriquet her famous guardian had given her, Belle et Bonne (Beautiful and Warmhearted).

Betsy often went to the opera with Madame de Villette, and she went on outings with David Bailie Warden, shopping for books and for gifts for friends at home. But she formed her deepest friendship with another outsider, Lady Sydney Morgan, who, like Betsy, had been welcomed into salon culture. This Irish novelist and travel writer was already a celebrity in Paris when she and Betsy met. And although Sydney's happy marriage and her literary reputation set her apart from Betsy, the two formed a friendship that lasted for decades.

Sydney's literary talents had emerged quite early. By the time she was fourteen, this daughter of an impoverished actor had produced a volume of poems. In the same year that Betsy became a mother, Sydney published her first novel. Two years later her second book, *The Wild Irish Girl,* established her reputation as one of Ireland's leading authors. In 1812 she married a physician, Sir Thomas Charles Morgan, who Betsy once declared was the only man who ever understood her. After her marriage, Sydney alienated many readers by making her liberal views on politics and religion public. Betsy did not share her friend's politics, but she admired her stubborn independence. Sydney admired Betsy's independent spirit as well, but she sensed the bitterness and disappointment that underlay her friend's hostility to America and to marriage.

Over her lifetime, Betsy had few true female confidantes. Although she exchanged friendly letters with Dolley Madison and Eliza Godefroy, she did not share her most deeply felt emotions with them. But Betsy would share her moods of both despair and satisfaction with Sydney, who she confessed she admired and loved more than anyone else. With Sydney, she did not feel it necessary to be always charming and obliging or witty, as she did with most of the wealthy aristocrats and impoverished intellectuals whose favor she had won. Nor did she feel compelled to fill her letters to Sydney exclusively with accounts of her triumphs, as she did in correspondence with her father, family, and friends. In her many letters to Sydney, she could be herself, admitting she was "very tired of suffering," whether it was from illnesses or from bitter memories. If the confidences she shared in this correspondence over the years often bore the mark of nineteenth-century romanticism, with its emphasis on ennui, sadness, and tragic experiences, still they revealed a Betsy that few others ever saw.

With the exception of Warden and the Gallatins, Betsy had few contacts with Americans in Paris. She preferred to ignore overtures by the American tourists who had begun to fill the streets of the city. She found "their whining . . . at the corruption of European morals" tedious and believed that they sought introductions to the Parisian literati and nobility from her solely so that they could confirm the superiority of their "primitive simplicity & republican opinions." She assured her cousin John Spear Smith that she did not care if these American visitors were angry at her icy rejection of their company: "I shall survive all their criticism as long as I can associate with those persons whom they rail against." She had found the French "quite as good as Americans," indeed better, for they were less hypocritical, no more selfish, and definitely more amiable. In fact, France was altogether superior to the United States, for "there is quite as much natural affection, more friendship, at least as much disinterestedness as in our Country, where are found such lofty pretentions & sentimental acting."

Betsy's success in Paris made her even more loath to return to America, "where no pleasures no hopes await me." In Paris she could forget her husband's desertion, her father's rejection, and the dreariness of Baltimore. Here in the City of Light, "the weight of existence is lightened by intercourse with the world & one's unhappy recollections are suspended—there is no time here to reflect on a future which has no hopes to enliven it, or to deplore an experience of life which has stripped it of all illusion." She knew her income was too meager to remain in France, and yet few cords bound her to America: "Ah! That Country can claim no gratitude from me for I never experienced its favors. Bitter are its recollections—deplorable the anticipation of returning to it."

When she spoke of America, Betsy could conjure up only

her deadening image of "those long wearisome winter Evenings varied only by the entrance of tea Equipage minding the Fire & handing round Apples & nuts." The tedium was unbearable, for "imagination, feeling, taste intelligence are not only super-fluous to such a situation, they irritate a mind without amusement & render the load of existence as insupportable [and] as disgusting." She knew there were "dull persons" able to support this stagnation of life with patience, but it promised nothing but "the most acute of all pains to one of an animated disposition." After only a few months in Paris, she believed that for her it was "the only habitable place on earth." The only question was, How long could she really remain there?

Increasingly, this realization that she must return to the "waste of life" that defined existence in America depressed Betsy. She dreaded returning to a world in which men and women were "shut up in our melancholy country houses where we vegetate for months alone." In truth, the thought of the long wearisome winter evenings that awaited her made her physically ill. By the spring of 1817, she suffered from congested lungs. Her doctor warned that her liver was also affected. Back home in Dublin by this time, Sydney Morgan worried about her friend's "tone of tristesse and suffering" and urged Betsy to come to Ireland. She wished she could magically transport her American friend to her home, where she could "nurse you out of your illness & laugh you out of your ennui." But Betsy knew such a trip would further drain her resources and only briefly delay the inevitable.

On September 12, 1817, the inevitable came. Betsy sailed from Le Havre for New York on the *Maria Theresa*. Only a few days after her departure, James McIlhiny sent her a letter that was typically judgmental in tone. She suffered, he wrote, because she had clung to "an Eroneous [*sic*] notion of things as Respected yourself . . . your ideas soar'd too high for anything in your own Country which of course must have given offence to all around you & consequently must have been Disagreeable to your own Family." If Betsy would only adjust her expectations to fit the realities of life in Baltimore, she could find a measure of contentment. "How happy would Millions of Millions be," he reminded her, "if they had the same Means that you have in your Power."

Chapter Ten

"For This Life There Is Nothing but Disappointment"

B etsy took no consolation from the thought that "Millions of Millions" might envy her situation. True, she had sufficient means to live comfortably in Baltimore, but could she find a way to accumulate enough to return to Europe? It seemed unlikely. Betsy had returned to an America that was in the throes of a financial crisis as severe as her own. Agricultural prices had fallen dramatically, especially in the cotton states, and this had a ripple effect: credit grew tight, and foreclosures on farms across the country began. Soon banks began to fail. In 1819 a full-fledged panic would grip the nation, but already in 1817 fortunes were being lost, and Betsy's uncle, Samuel Smith, was among those who were ruined in the first wave of the crisis. Although her own cautious investment habits ensured that she was not wiped out, her resources seemed inadequate to fulfill her desires.

Betsy understood both her own and the nation's economic situation far better than many middle-class or elite women. For whether her fortunes rose or fell, she had played an active role in managing her own finances ever since her pension from Napoleon began in 1808. She had followed the economic upswings and downturns both at home and abroad with a concentration that matched her father's. In her careful husbanding of her wealth, in her active study of the relative worth of stocks and bonds and real estate investments, she would reveal time after time how deeply she had become implicated in the very moneymaking American culture that she criticized. Her letters to her father, brothers, and the family members managing her investments at home were regularly filled with sharp questions about the relative merits of stocks, real estate properties, and government bonds. She kept detailed records of her expenditures, weighing the cost of repairs to her rental properties and measuring the returns on treasury bonds. She followed political developments with a watchful eye and often commented on their impact on economic conditions. An ungenerous father and a faithless husband had forced financial independence upon her, and her survival required her to be as clever about wealth as any of the men whose brains she declared were clogged with thoughts of commerce.

Betsy was probably unaware of the inherent contradiction between her behavior and her ideology, but she was all too painfully aware of her misery in Baltimore. Despite the danger that she would have to deplete her capital, she was determined to return to Europe as soon as possible. A second trip abroad was necessary, she decided, not simply for her sanity but for Bo's future. In 1818 he was a young man of fourteen and in need of a proper education. When her good friend the Swiss-born Albert Gallatin suggested she consider educating Bo in Geneva, she saw a chance to justify an escape from the tedium of her native city. She and Bo would go to Europe, where she would enroll him in one of Switzerland's excellent schools. The decision was a bit reckless, given her financial situation, but the ennui and despair that had settled over her made her bold.

By May 1819, as the economic depression deepened across the United States, Betsy and Bo were on their way to Europe. The most convenient route for mother and son would have been to travel through France to Geneva. But to Betsy's surprise, the French government refused to grant Bo a passport. Unlike his mother, Bo carried Bonaparte blood in his veins, and this was enough to disturb the officials of the restored monarchy. The fact that Bo bore a striking resemblance to his notorious uncle, Napoleon, hardened the government's resolve. A roundabout route—and for added security, false identities—was necessary. Thus in June 1819 a "Mrs. Patterson" and her son "Edward Patterson" arrived in Amsterdam. From there they made their way through Germany to Switzerland.

Arriving in Geneva, Betsy was immediately convinced of the wisdom of Gallatin's advice. She wasted no time enrolling her son in a school and finding accommodations for herself. She settled into a small but pleasant apartment in town, big enough for Bo to spend weekends with her.

Betsy was enthusiastic about her son's new situation, but Bo was far less satisfied. Unlike his mother, Jerome Napoleon Bonaparte had a strong and conflict-free attachment to his grandfather William Patterson. William, in turn, had come to dote on his grandson, so much so that he had made the unusually generous gesture of paying for Bo's schooling in Maryland during Betsy's first trip abroad. Despite the novelty of his own first trip to Europe, Bo was homesick for his grandfather and for the comfortable, predictable life in Baltimore that William had

provided. He was soon assuring his grandfather that he would
return home as soon as his education was complete. "I shall
hasten over to America," he wrote, admitting that he regretted
ever leaving it.

Bo's longing for home, genuine though it might be, was not
based entirely on his emotional attachment to family, friends,
and familiar places. Like his father, Bo was growing into a young
man given to extravagances, but his mother's limited resources
required life on a tight budget. He quickly learned that he could
not live in Geneva in as grand a style as he had in Baltimore.
Betsy, who lived a relatively Spartan life in a four-room apartment, with only one servant, was willing to sacrifice in order to
provide for Bo's tuition, lodgings, and a host of gentlemanly les-
sons like fencing and riding. But she was not willing to indulge
her son's whims. She was, in fact, appalled by his cavalier attitude toward money, especially her money. She found it necessary to lower his expectations: when, for instance, he asked for a
horse, she bought him a dog instead. Providing a home for this
pet, Betsy reasoned, would be far less expensive than renting
space in a stable, even if she did indulge the dog with sheets and
pillows for its bed.

With Bo settled at school, Betsy could investigate the city's
social possibilities. She discovered, to her delight, that many of
the Russian and Polish aristocrats who had befriended her in
Paris were now in residence in Geneva. Among them were the
philanthropist Karl Viktor von Bonstetten, Princess Alexandra
Gallitzin, and the aging Nicolay Demidov, rumored to be the
richest man in Europe, whom Betsy seemed to genuinely care

for and admire. Delighted to see their American friend, this circle of Europeans happily included Betsy in their endless rounds
of dinners, parties, balls, and amateur theatrical performances.
Writing to his grandfather, Bo reported that "Mamma goes out
nearly every night to a party or a ball."

Whatever Bo thought of his mother's social life, Betsy found
it a tonic. Her renewed popularity seemed to dispel her melancholy and restore her health. The contrast with her dreary
life in Baltimore was obvious to her: now thirty-five, she was
considered old in America; but in Europe's aristocratic circles,
where wit and charm were valued in a woman, she knew she
could remain a belle well into her fifties or sixties. Here, in the
company of Demidov and his friends, she could feel the suffo-
cating constraints of America's emerging cult of domesticity fall
away; among these aristocrats, she could indulge in sociability
elevated to an art form. She could act, in short, upon a public
stage rather than be confined to the private world of parlor and
nursery. Bo conveyed her delight in a letter to William: "She
says she looks full ten years younger than she is, and if she had
not so large a son she could pass for five and twenty years old."

Betsy ignored her own countrymen and -women living in
Geneva, just as she had avoided them during her earlier sojourns
in London and Paris. Her contempt for American tourists
remained intense; she believed their sole purpose in coming
to Europe was to affirm their belief that American culture was
morally superior to that of a decadent Old World. And yet as
contemptuous as she was of her fellow Americans, she refused
to allow Europeans to criticize or mock them. One of the most

widely recounted anecdotes of Betsy's brilliant wit involved a dinner table exchange with an Englishman who spoke ill of American manners. He asked her if she was surprised by the judgment of a British travel writer who had concluded that Americans were vulgarians. It was a view Betsy herself had often expressed. But she replied, "I was not surprised. Were the Americans descendants of the Indians and Esquimaux, I should have been. But being direct descendants of the English, nothing is more natural than that they be vulgarians." Clearly, like expatriates in every century, Betsy Patterson Bonaparte believed that only she enjoyed the privilege of criticizing the country she had fled.

The only American Betsy did befriend was the German American fur trader John Jacob Astor, a man whose rags-to-riches story was different only in scale from that of her father, William Patterson. Like Betsy, Astor had come to Switzerland to place one of his children, a daughter, in school. Betsy sensed that Astor and her father shared more in common than an immigrant past and a prosperous present: their great wealth had brought them little happiness. Betsy might have been talking about William Patterson as much as Astor when she wrote: "He seems, poor man, afflicted with possession of a fortune which he had greater pleasure in amassing than he can ever find in spending." But Astor's friendship had important consequences for both her and her son, for it was Astor who brought Betsy to the attention of the Bonaparte family in Italy.

In the autumn of 1819, John Jacob Astor made a trip to Rome, where members of Napoleon's family had found sanctuary after the emperor's exile. Here he met the family matriarch, Letizia, as well as her brother, Cardinal Fesch, and Jérôme's notorious sister Pauline, now the Princess Borghese, whose beauty and sexual infidelities were legendary in Europe. When Astor told Pauline and her mother that Betsy and Bo were in Geneva, the strong-willed Madame Mère and her profligate daughter grew excited. They were eager, they told him, to meet Jérôme's American wife and her son.

In March 1820, Astor dutifully reported their interest to Betsy, but he warned her not to trust any member of the family. Soon afterward Betsy's good friend Lady Sydney Morgan and her husband stopped by to see her in Geneva, on their way back to Dublin from Rome. Sydney confirmed the fur merchant's judgment. She told Betsy frankly that it would be madness to take the child on a visit to Italy. The Bonapartes were quixotic and self-centered, Sydney observed; they were simply not to be trusted. In fact, Sydney was certain that Pauline had ulterior motives for inviting them to visit: she hated both her brother Jérôme and his wife, Catherine, and any contact with Betsy and her son would be a slap in their faces. It was best, Betsy's friends agreed, to avoid contact with the Bonaparte family.

Betsy was uncertain what course of action to take. She had sound reasons to ignore the Bonapartes' invitation, chief among them the expense of a trip to Rome and the need to take Bo out of school. She was especially hesitant to disrupt her son's education on the vague chance that the family, as Pauline broadly hinted, intended to provide an inheritance, or at least an allowance, for him. Knowing Bo's tendency toward extravagance, she also worried about the impact of Pauline's lifestyle on her son. Writing to her father in April 1820, Betsy sounded decidedly like one of those practical, conscientious Americans whom she so often held up to contempt. "If I took my son to live in a palace," she wrote, "he would naturally prefer pleasure to study."

Her concern revealed a slowly emerging ambivalence about the relative merits of aristocratic idleness and the middle-class work ethic. She was willing to sacrifice, to live a Spartan existence, in order to provide Bo the best education possible, but in turn she expected him to work hard and to excel in all his subjects. She did not hesitate to remind him of the "necessity of application to his studies," and she regularly asked his instructors for reports on his progress. As his mother, she would take all necessary steps to protect him from exposure to the style of life that his father and Pauline embraced, but in the end, the responsibility for mastering Latin, mathematics, chemistry, physics, history, and geography, as well as the cultured arts of fencing, dancing, and drawing, was his own. "If he should prove ignorant and insignificant," she told William, "the fault will not be mine."

Betsy's motives for providing Bo an elite education were, on the surface, contradictory. She wanted her son to acquire the cultured manners and the sophistication that she thought were necessary for him to marry into the European nobility. But at the same time she wanted his school years to equip him for a profession such as law or medicine. She fervently believed that he must be ready to make his way in the world if fortune did not smile on him. As she told William, "without an education he would find himself condemned to dependence on the caprice of others." But Betsy saw no contradiction in putting forward these two competing goals. Her own experience as a young woman had taught her to be cautious, to expect little good fortune in life, and to develop self-reliance. If fortune—in the form of a brilliant marriage—did not provide for her son, then he must be prepared to provide for himself. Such an alternative would have been unthinkable to the European aristocrats she admired. But Betsy had grown up in a country that embraced meritocracy and promised opportunity to men of ability, training, and ambition. Thousands of miles from Baltimore, Betsy Patterson Bonaparte was thinking like an American.

For the moment, she decided not to accept the Bonaparte invitation to bring Bo to Rome. In a letter to Pauline, she explained that her decision rested on a reluctance to interrupt his schooling. She signed this letter "Elizabeth Patterson." In the meantime, however, she decided to assess the fortunes of the Bonaparte family—and the likelihood that she and Bo could benefit from their wealth. She had long ago abandoned any expectations that her former husband would provide for his son. Jérôme had contributed little if anything to Bo's education or maintenance, and as she and everyone else knew, the king of Westphalia remained as recklessly extravagant as he had been in his youth. As Betsy put it, he "spends everything he can get hold of, and will keep up kingly state until his expended means leave him a beggar." She stopped short of accusing Jérôme of having a cruel nature. He did not use money as a weapon the way her father did. "I believe he is not as bad-hearted as many people think," she wrote, "and that many of his faults and much of his bad conduct proceed from extravagance and folly." Jérôme's sin was not his abuse of power; it was simply the weakness of his character.

Betsy also doubted that any support would come from the Bonaparte family living in Rome. True, Madame Mère seemed to be "a woman of sense and great fortitude," but much of her wealth had gone to pay her irresponsible children's many bills. Little of her fortune remained, and Betsy assumed it would go to her remaining adult children. The Princess Borghese had a great fortune, but her past promises to provide generously for a family member or friend had proven unreliable. Betsy knew less about the finances or temperaments of the remaining Bonaparte brothers, Lucien, Louis, and Joseph. She did know that she and Lucien shared one thing in common: Napoleon's fury at what he deemed an inappropriate marriage. And she knew that Joseph was now residing in America on an elegant estate built with the gold and silver he had buried for safekeeping when the empire collapsed. But she could not imagine a role that any of these men would play in her son's future.

Betsy had weighed the benefits of a trip to Rome—and found they were few. Still, she could not lay the notion of a trip south entirely to rest. Her desire to show her son off to the Bonapartes was strong. She was confident Bo would make a good impression on his father's family, for he spoke excellent French, had fine manners, and was, as a friend of Nancy Spear put it, "amiable & remarkably Sensible." And his resemblance to Napoleon, which had so troubled the French monarchy's officials, was certain to win him their affection. By the fall of 1821, Betsy had set aside her doubts and misgivings and decided to take the trip after all.

In Rome, Betsy and Bo were greeted with enthusiasm.

Madame Mère showered her grandson with gifts and money, and Cardinal Fesch announced that he had amended his will to include the young man. But it was the beautiful Pauline, whose second marriage to Prince Camillo Borghese had provided her with the means to live and entertain lavishly, who offered the most dazzling welcome. She doted on Bo, giving him great sums of money for new clothes and promising him a sizable annual allowance when he married.

Pauline seemed equally charmed by Betsy, showering her with gifts of jewelry and an elaborate ball gown. Betsy was momentarily overcome by these acts of generosity, which seemed so in keeping with Pauline's oversize personality. Indeed, everything about the Princess Borghese was larger than life, from her palatial villa, so opulent that Sydney Morgan referred to its style as "beyond beyond," to the life-size sculpture of herself reclining in the nude, created by the Italian artist Antonio Canova, that greeted guests as they entered her home. The nude sculpture suggested that modesty was not one of Pauline's virtues, and her idiosyncratic behavior left no doubt in anyone's mind that she preferred to shock her guests rather than put them at ease. She was known to receive guests wearing a demi-negligee. A German visitor recorded having a conversation with Pauline while a young page, kneeling at the hostess's feet, pulled down her stockings and garter to wash and dry her feet. If Betsy had once disturbed the peace of American matrons by appearing in a dress that revealed her "bubbies," Pauline's daily behavior made Betsy's brief flaunting of convention seem a timid endeavor.

Betsy may have been disturbed by Pauline's impropriety. But

she was euphoric at the welcome she and Bo received. Still, the warnings given by Astor and her good friend Sydney, that the Bonapartes were both sly and mercurial in their affections, remained in the corner of her mind. Were they sincere? Would they keep their promises? All her nagging doubts seemed to dissolve when the family suggested a marriage between Bo and his uncle Joseph Bonaparte's daughter Charlotte.

Joseph Bonaparte was the oldest of Letizia and Carlo Buonaparte's sons. In 1808 Napoleon named him king of Naples, and later he became king of Spain. After Napoleon's defeat at Waterloo, however, Joseph fled with his family to Switzerland, managing to take with him a sizable treasure in Spanish gold and jewels, much of which he buried near his Swiss château. Joseph then made his way, without his family, to America, where he purchased a large estate in Bordentown, New Jersey, known as Point Breeze. He soon sent his trusted friend and secretary, Louis Mailliard, back to Europe to retrieve the remaining treasure. Mailliard returned to America with the treasure and Joseph's two daughters, Zénaïde and Charlotte. Joseph's wife, Julie, remained in Europe because of poor health. By the time the Bonapartes of Rome proposed the marriage, Joseph, now calling himself the Comte de Survilliers, and his daughters were comfortably settled in a beautiful home at Point Breeze.

The proposed marriage of her son to one of the *comte*'s daughters was more than Betsy had ever hoped for: an alliance that would secure Bo's place in the Bonaparte family and tacitly confirm the legitimacy of her own marriage to Jérôme. And, because the family knew Jérôme could not be counted on to do a father's duty, Madame Mère and Pauline pledged to provide

Bo with the funds needed to support a wife. Jérôme might be "entirely ruined, his fortune, capital, income, everything spent," but his son's future seemed suddenly rosy.

At the age of sixteen, Bo probably did not have marriage on his mind. But the fact that his intended bride-to-be lived in America pleased him greatly. He was eager to get home any way he could. Writing to his grandfather William, he made his preference for American society plain: "Since I have been in Europe I have dined with princes and princesses and all the great people of Europe, but I have never tasted a dish as much to my taste as the roast beef and beef-steaks I ate on South Street." Betsy's fear that Bo would succumb to the aristocratic life of luxury—and in Pauline's case, decadence—that now surrounded him had not proved entirely groundless; her son did indeed love a life of ease, but he wanted to live it in America.

To Bo's delight, it was decided that he should travel home to confer with his uncle Joseph and make the acquaintance of the young girl who would be his wife. While she waited to learn the outcome of the marriage plan, Betsy filled her letters to William with her thoughts on the most practical of matters: the financial settlement Joseph should grant his daughter and her husband-to-be. She wanted a prenuptial agreement that ensured Bo an ample share of Charlotte's wealth should she die before him. She also meant to insist that half of the hundred-thousand-dollar marriage gift that Joseph was said to be offering his daughter be settled directly on Bo. She did not think this demand was outrageous, for she now knew that Joseph's daughter stood to inherit far more than this wedding gift. She estimated that Charlotte would receive half a million dollars from her father's estate and a considerable sum from her mother's as well. Although she might be willing to compromise on some of the prenuptial terms, Betsy was determined to see an ironclad legal agreement reached. "There is no knowing how marriages may turn out," she wrote her father—a sad truth that no one knew better than Elizabeth Patterson Bonaparte.

Bo's marriage to Charlotte would satisfy all the wishes for her son that Betsy had harbored for so long. It would not only ensure Bo's place within the Bonaparte family and provide him with an ample income; it would also bring him a social position unequaled in America. As for love, she expressed nothing but contempt for those who believed such a transient emotion was the proper basis for marriage. Her own history had proven such an idea absurd. She asked William, whom Bo respected and looked up to, to "discourage all that tendency to romance and absurd falling in love which has been the ruin of your own family."

As the weeks and months dragged on, however, no news of an engagement arrived in Rome. Betsy found herself preparing for the worst. She had to admit that even before Bo left for America, her relationship with the Bonapartes had begun to sour. And in the months of waiting that followed, the tensions had increased. Pauline's behavior became erratic: first she demanded the return of the ball gown she had given Betsy; then she pressed Betsy to accept it as a gift once more. Worse was to come: Pauline's promises to provide for Bo simply evaporated. The only consolation Betsy could take was that the childless Pauline had treated Bo "exactly as she has done all her other nephews—that is, promised, and then retracted." When Jérôme, who maintained a villa in Florence, made it clear that he resented the family opening its arms to his former wife, Pauline staunchly denied that she had invited Betsy to Rome and loudly announced that she wished her unwelcome visitor would return to Geneva. In the end, Betsy concluded that "all that has been said of her is not half what she deserves—neither hopes of legacies, nor any expectation can make any one support her whims, which are so extraordinary as to make it impossible not to believe her mad."

The situation had become intolerable for Betsy, and she returned to Switzerland, where she began to steel herself for the end to all her dreams. The bitterness she felt at her own past misfortune rose to the surface, coloring her judgment of her son's future and her own. It was clear: there were to be no happy endings. In a letter to her father on December 21, 1821, she had declared that the happiest people "are those who support misfortune best." In 1822 she was resigned to numbering herself among those unhappy happiest people.

In October 1821, before the Roman debacle, Betsy had written a long letter to her father about her finances. "It is generally my luck to be cheated in every way," she noted with heavy resignation. She was referring to the exorbitant charges she suffered when drawing on funds through bankers in Amsterdam. But she might just as well have been talking about her experiences with the Bonaparte family. The only one who had ever dealt honestly with her, she knew, was Napoleon.

Chapter Eleven

"That Was My American Wife"

While the debacle of Bo's proposed marriage played itself out, Betsy began a peripatetic life in Europe, dividing her time between Geneva, Florence, the coast of France, and Paris. Although the Russian-Polish contingent had relocated to Florence, Geneva still boasted a number of interesting friends. She could spend evenings with the famous economist and historian Jean-Charles-Leonard de Sismondi and his family and enjoy the sparkling conversation, and the admiration, of the elderly philosopher Karl Viktor von Bonstetten. Although he was married and nearing eighty, Bonstetten enjoyed a flirtation with Betsy. "You may not have reigned in Westphalia," he is said to have told her, "but then you are the Queen of all hearts, which is much better!" But Demidov and his circle were a magnet, and Betsy found herself spending more of her time in Florence. Here she could lose herself in the seemingly endless rounds of parties and theatrical productions that Demidov hosted.

The only sour note was that Jérôme had also relocated to Italy, and when he was in Florence, Betsy felt compelled to stay away. Their one chance meeting was enough for her. They encountered each other in a gallery at the Pitti Palace, Jérôme with his wife, the portly Catherine, on his arm, Betsy without an escort. Not a word passed between them, but Betsy heard her former husband remark to his entourage, "Did you see? That was my American wife." Awkward though the moment was, it may have given Betsy a touch of satisfaction. Jérôme was still a dandy, but he was now heavier, his features more pronounced and sharper, his hair graying. Betsy, on the other hand, remained as beautiful as ever.

That enduring beauty attracted suitors wherever Betsy went. Even Pauline's husband, the Prince Borghese, vainly attempted to make Betsy his mistress. Rumors that she was about to marry one smitten suitor or another continued to spread across the Atlantic. Letters from Baltimore asked if she had already married Lord William Russell, a prominent English liberal some eighteen years her senior, and if not, when was the wedding to be? Whatever hopes Russell entertained, they would be dashed, just as the desires of another Englishman, Henry Edward Fox, would come to nothing. When the young Mr. Fox failed to win Betsy, his ardor turned to enmity, and his journal began to bristle with sour-grapes comments on her "vulgar" manners, "the extreme profligacy of her opinions," and even the "indecency of her expressions." Unlike the bitter Fox, most of the men who courted Betsy conceded defeat graciously, content to settle for friendship or to admire her from afar. Sir George Dallas was typical of those who wooed her—and lost. His affection for Betsy continued from a distance. After his return to England from Italy, he confessed to his mother: "I every Day miss Mrs Pattersons agreeable, Spirituelle, naïve Conversation and like a Harp unstrung for want of being play'd on, I feel I am losing both my tones and my own powers in this way—she roused me."

Yet Betsy remained alone. This was not, she assured her correspondents, because she was waiting to fall in love before marrying. She declared that romance was a concept embraced only by fools, the young—and Americans. "The land of romance," she observed to her father, "is now only to be found on the other side of the Atlantic. . . . Love in a cottage is even out of fashion in novels." She marveled at this persistence of romance in her native country, where "foolish and unreflecting youths" plunged headlong into disastrous marriages. The blame, as Betsy saw it, lay not simply in the "whimsical self-will" of young men and women but in the "absurd folly of parents" who did not prevent mistakes from being made.

Betsy had not married Jérôme with dreams of "love in a cottage," of course, but surely her description of the "foolish and unreflecting" youths who rushed into marriage thinking only of the present moment was more autobiographical than sociological. And surely her condemnation of American parents contained an implicit reprimand of her father for failing to prevent her own folly. Regret and anger underlay her cynicism.

The impetuous young woman who believed that the love she and Jérôme shared would solve all problems, dispel all anger, and conquer all objections was gone. In her place was an Elizabeth Patterson Bonaparte who viewed marriage as a strictly social and economic institution. Its participants, she declared, should be guided by two simple rules: first, marry up or marry an equal, but never marry beneath one's social rank; and second, if a suitable partner could not be found, "the next best thing to making a good match is not to make a bad one." It was this credo, not fading looks or aging, that made Betsy declare it "improbable that I shall ever marry." For as Betsy knew, her own "rank" was anomalous: she was an outcast of an imperial house, itself now brought low by exile and military defeat. But she had once been a Bonaparte, and her pride in how high she had risen made it impossible for her to be content with a man less prestigious than the current king of Westphalia. She put her position succinctly to William in 1829: "No consideration could have induced me to marry any one thereafter, having married the brother of an emperor." If William considered her dilemma a creation of her own pride, she saw it as a simple reality. "It would be impossible," she told her father, "for me ever to bend my spirit to marry any one who had been my equal before my marriage."

An astute observer might have declared that the old saw was probably true: a cynic was only a romantic who had been hurt. But in the 1820s, it is unlikely that Betsy could have discerned that disappointment, embarrassment, and disillusionment, more than pride or reason, had shaped her condemnation of "love in a cottage." She did know this, however: she would do all in her power to prevent her own child from making the same mistake.

It had become clear by 1823 that Bo was not fated for a union with a Bonaparte. Charlotte Bonaparte would indeed marry a cousin, but it would not be Betsy's son. Wary of an alliance with a branch of the family whose legitimacy was clouded, Joseph had opted to marry his daughter to his brother Louis's eldest son, Napoleon. Joseph was fond of Bo, but he preferred to be safe rather than sorry in establishing lasting family ties. It was becoming equally clear that for Bo, no suitable alternative to Charlotte was likely to appear. Thus Betsy assumed Bo must remain a bachelor. The issue being settled—in her mind, at least—they must focus all their attention on Bo's education and his selection of a future career. Writing to her father, she laid out her goals: "We must instill ambition in him, keep him from marrying too low, and give him a sense of economy."

Betsy was no stranger to ambition, and her own "sense of economy" was by now second nature. "Disappointments," she wrote, "teach prudence," and over the years she had learned "the high value of money, and the importance of increasing one's fortune." For most of her adult life, Elizabeth Patterson Bonaparte had scrimped and saved, living in respectable but modest quarters when she was in Europe and often relying on her wealthier friends to provide her with food and entertainment. On several occasions, she had politely refused to take up residence in more elegant surroundings, even when they were offered to her at no cost, because the upkeep of a carriage or a staff of servants would drain her resources. On other occasions, she had reluctantly moved in with friends who were able to share the costs involved. She knew, she told her father, that many considered her "almost a miser," but she refused to live beyond her means. She kept a careful, perhaps excessively careful, record of all her expenditures, large and small. The only exception to this constant, careful husbanding of her money that bordered on the obsessive was her willingness to provide her son a fine education.

Betsy often worried that her own brothers' spendthrift behavior would influence Bo. At other times, she feared that her own unceasing efforts to instill responsibility and ambition in him had had the reverse effect, for as she observed, "young people are often perverse and self-willed." And the thought was always there that he had inherited his father's impulse to spend all he had—and far more. Whatever the reason, it was becoming clear that Bo was not cut from the same cloth as his mother. As he grew older, he became less rather than more ambitious and more inclined to indulge himself; he was, in truth, a spoiled young man who loved comfort and ease. Still, he dutifully bowed to his mother's wishes and followed the necessary steps to get into Harvard College. He spent eight months working with a tutor to improve his grasp of Greek. At last, in February 1823, he was admitted to what Betsy considered America's finest school.

Thus far Betsy had enjoyed better luck in directing her son's choices than William had ever enjoyed in directing hers. But Bo's continuing extravagance troubled her. To her amazement and alarm, she discovered that he had managed to run up a bill of $2,150 during his first fifteen months back in America. Searching to understand the source of this prodigal behavior, she placed the blame on his grandfather. Once she had seen Baltimore businessmen like William Patterson as boring and consumed with accumulating money; now she concluded that their sins were greed, dishonesty, and financial profligacy.

But William, too, lectured his grandson on his excessive spending at Harvard. Bo resented what he considered their badgering. "However advantageous I may conceive a college education to be for me," he wrote William in March 1824, "I should prefer giving it up . . . rather than to hear these continual and uninterrupted complaints about my expenses." He insisted that he was "doing all in my power to give you satisfaction." But in one week he had received three letters from his mother and one from William, "all teeming with reproaches." He would live within the budget of $1,000 that his mother now set for him, he declared, even if it meant he could not afford to go home to Baltimore at the holidays.

Bo's character flaws could not be laid solely at the feet of his father, his grandfather, or Baltimore's capitalist culture. In truth, Betsy had created her own monster: years of assuring her son that he was special, that the Bonaparte blood running in his veins set him above most people, had shaped Bo's character as surely as his father's or grandfather's example had done.

Although Bo's extravagance got him into trouble with his mother, a different type of youthful indiscretion got him into trouble with the Harvard authorities. In 1824 he and several other students were temporarily suspended. In a long letter dated August 16, he did his best to explain the suspension to his grandfather. He had gone to a meeting of a student organization at which alcoholic punch was served. The organization was legitimate; the drinking was forbidden. All the students involved, including Bo, were punished with a ninety-day suspension. Betsy had just arrived in America when she got this news. She hurried to Massachusetts, furious with both Bo and the Harvard officials who had suspended him. When she calmed down, she realized that the affair had a positive outcome: it offered her a rare opportunity to spend a few months with her son. It was probably the happiest episode in their relationship.

When Bo returned to college, Betsy made her way to Balti-more. Almost immediately she found herself in a tense confron-tation with William. Her father assumed that she had returned for good, but if this pleased him, he did not show it by welcom-ing his daughter back into his home. In fact, he did not want her in his house at all. Where once he had insisted that she take over her mother's domestic duties, now he urged her to take up residence in one of her rental properties. William claimed this arrangement would be best for both of them, since Betsy's presence had always caused "confusion" in the past. But Betsy suspected another motive: one of William's mistresses was there to provide him all the company and care he needed.

William's response to her homecoming made Betsy eager to return to Europe as soon as possible. But first she had to review her finances. By 1824, this tendency to watch her invest-ments like a hawk had become second nature. Unlike most of Baltimore's business community, she was determined to avoid making any investments linked to the war now raging between France and Spain. The conflict had been good for American trade, but it did not prompt her to put her money in shipping. She would not gamble, as most of the local merchants seemed willing to do, that the war would expand into a general Euro-pean conflict. She considered this sort of speculating a fool's errand, driven by greed. She was equally skittish about other avenues of investment, for the panics and depressions of recent years had made a deep impression on her. As she told her father, "I have no confidence in the banks, insurance companies, road stocks, or, in short, in any stock in Baltimore." When confidence in the state and federal governments was fully restored, she intended to put the bulk of her money in their bonds.

No matter how shrewdly or cautiously she invested, Betsy could not consider herself financially secure. She did not have enough, she told Sydney Morgan, to return to Europe—and yet she knew that if she remained in Baltimore, she faced a lifetime of ennui, she lamented to her Irish friend. She must do as she had done for almost a decade: tighten her belt, eliminate luxuries, and escape the city of her birth. In June 1825 she sailed to Europe. This time she would not return to America for nine years.

Betsy arrived at Le Havre that summer. Although she was certainly happier to be in Europe than in Maryland, she conceded that the excitement of living abroad had begun to fade. Even Paris, despite its balls and dinner parties, had lost some of its luster, for both "Belle et Bonne" and De Staël were dead, and Sydney Morgan had returned home. Perhaps the greater problem was that Betsy Bonaparte was no longer the only American celebrity abroad. The Caton sisters, granddaughters of the richest man in Maryland, Charles Carroll, had recently become the toast of England. News that they were being feted by the Duke of Wellington, as she had once been, roused an intense jealousy in Betsy. So too did the financial support these women received from their doting grandfather. The Caton women were said to be openly seeking husbands among the English aristocracy, and the marriage settlements he would provide made them attractive to many a titled Englishman.

Betsy did nothing to hide a contempt that others, rightly, viewed as envy. While she economized, the Catons enjoyed every luxury. It was, she wrote, her deepest wish that the duke would tire of these "*mere* adventurers and swindlers" and of their pressure on him to find them suitable husbands. Emily and Louisa Caton, she wrote, were nothing more than "ignorant, unprincipled asses" who should never have left America. They tarnished the reputation of other women seeking cultural asylum in Europe. However, her wrath was most intensely focused on Marianne, the widow of her own brother, Robert Patterson. It was a great blow to Betsy when Marianne married Wellington's older brother, Lord Wellesley, in the fall of 1825. Wellesley was both old and in debt, yet the marriage was hailed as a brilliant triumph for his American bride. Years later Betsy's hostility to the Catons was undimmed. In 1867 she called them "the most pernicious foes of my life," but their only crime seems to have been their good fortune.

Betsy's focus on the fate of the Caton sisters was as brief as it was intense. By 1826 she had a more pressing issue to face: the Bonapartes, including her former husband, wanted her to allow Bo to return to Italy. Jérôme, along with other members of the Bonaparte family, had kept in touch with Bo throughout his college years, and Jérôme had even managed to contribute twice to his Harvard expenses. The king of Westphalia now expressed a desire to meet his oldest son. Betsy decided it was her duty to make this possible. If she denied Bo the opportunity, he might resent it. "I should pass . . . for a very unfeeling parent if I do not let him see his father," she wrote to William, a man she believed was all too often unfeeling. Worse, he might reproach himself for failing to visit Jérôme.

But even before Bo set sail that May, Jérôme had begun to

have second thoughts about extending the invitation to his son. Perhaps he had acted too impulsively. If he welcomed Bo into his home, would it give the appearance of invalidating his marriage to Catherine? He did not wish to disturb the courts of Württemberg and Russia, whose generosity had long supported him. Fearing he had made a mistake, he sent a letter to Baltimore, warning that the meeting might, after all, be awkward for both father and son.

As usual, Jérôme was thinking largely of himself. In the letter, he took pains to assure Bo that he wanted to behave honorably. "My dear child," he wrote, "you are now a man, and I desire to place you in a natural position." But the rest of the sentence revealed Jérôme's characteristic eagerness to avoid any consequences of his actions. He wanted to acknowledge Bo "without, however, prejudicing in any way the condition of the queen and the princes, our children." As a solution, he suggested that Bo go to Leghorn, where he would receive instructions on a safe, neutral place for father and son to meet. Without any sense of the insults he had just delivered, Jérôme signed the letter, "Your affectionate father."

Bo knew nothing of this proposed change in plans; he had already set sail before his father's letter reached Baltimore. Arriving at Amsterdam, he made his way to Switzerland, where he met his mother, and together the two traveled on to Florence. Although the trip south was filled with beautiful sights and the hospitality of many of Betsy's friends, Bo's opinion of the relative merits of America and Europe did not change. In a letter to his grandfather, he confided what he could not reveal to his mother. "I have seen a great many things since my departure from home," he wrote, "but the more I see, the more firmly I am persuaded of the superiority of my own country, the more I desire to return to it and to remain in it." He had come to Europe to meet his father, but when "it is all over I shall settle myself quietly in America."

For William Patterson, Bo's preference for life in America was a triumph over Betsy. It was also a vindication of his position on Betsy's life choices. "I perceive that he is tired of Europe," he wrote to his daughter, "& expresses his anxiety of returning to this Country, this I do not wonder at for no one of an independent spirit could think of living in Europe after having seen & experienced the happy state of this Country compared to any other in the world." In the long-running contest between father and daughter, Bo's future had become a prize. "As to your idea that it might be useful for Bo to spend another year in Europe . . . I am quite of a contrary opinion," William told Betsy, "& I think he has too much good sense not to think with me." Driving his point home, he added, "This is the only Country in which he can live with any satisfaction to himself & the less he sees or knows of the follies of Europe the better."

Betsy responded in kind, but William managed to have the last word. "You seem somewhat angry at my observations," he noted, "& insist on your own situation being greatly preferable to that of people in this Country who live in a quiet rational way, it is well you think as you do, but I doubt your sincerity in that respect, for I can see no rational ground for happiness in the kind of life you lead, it seems to me that a common housekeeper here who can indulge in going to Methodist meeting & attend to religious duties has a much better chance of Happiness both here & hereafter than those who pass their time in idle disapation [sic] as must be the case from representation of the state of society in Florence." Her father's reference to a "common housekeeper" surely inflamed Betsy, for she knew his own mistresses were drawn from that profession. When she later annotated this letter, Betsy listed these women and exposed her father's hypocrisy: "His own life moral & exempt from the pretense of Todd, Somer Wheeler immaculate not found out to be. Ah! Mr. Patterson afford example to accompany the above pious preception. He never believed in the truth of the Christian religion."

Bo was probably unaware of the contest for his soul being waged between his grandfather and his mother. But for the moment, his immersion in "the follies of Europe" could not be avoided if he wanted to meet his father and his father's family. Thus, while Betsy settled down in Florence for the winter, Bo continued south to Rome for a reunion with the Bonapartes living there. Then at the end of October, he traveled to the château of Lanciano, near Camerino, where his father lived with his wife; his two sons, Jérôme and Napoleon; and his daughter, Mathilde. The meeting was thus open rather than covert, for the concerns Jérôme had about his American son's reception had proved baseless. Catherine was gracious, and none of her royal relatives issued any complaints.

After two months Jérôme's entire family, Bo included, moved to Rome. Here Bo's disdain for his father's version of an aristocratic life emerged. "I am excessively tired of the way of living at my father's," he told William. "We breakfast between twelve and one o'clock, dine between six and seven, take tea between eleven and twelve at night, so that I seldom get to bed before half-past one o'clock in the morning." But it was not simply the late hours that troubled Bo; it was the lack of any meaningful activity during the day. The family simply gathered together in the parlor, "principally for the purpose of killing time." Bo's criticism did not spring from any desire to achieve greatness or make a significant contribution to society; rather, its roots were practical. His father spent more money than he had; he ought to be busy finding new sources of income. He ought, that is, to do as William Patterson and his fellow Baltimore merchants did: invest, buy, and sell—make money.

But Jérôme's extravagance, his living far beyond his means, his willingness to drain Madame Mère of her own dwindling fortune, was not simply a commentary on his character. Bo realized it had serious consequences for his own future. It meant that neither his Bonaparte grandmother nor his father would be able to provide for him even had they wanted to. The only sensible thing to do, Bo concluded, was "think of doing something for myself." And he added, "America is the only country where I can have an opportunity of getting forward."

Betsy might have agreed with Bo's conclusion but not with his solution. After two years of desultory study of the law, Bo found a less tedious route to wealth: he married it.

Chapter Twelve

"He Has Neither My Pride, My Ambition, nor My Love of Good Company"

B o's courtship of Susan May Williams had begun without Betsy's knowledge, and it had proceeded with the full support of William Patterson. Until now William had joined his daughter in advising Bo to remain a bachelor, but his motives stood at cross-purposes to his daughter's. Betsy hoped to prevent what she considered an unsuitable marriage outside the European aristocracy; William hoped to prevent his grandson from marrying into it. The Bonapartes, he told Bo, lived in the past, clinging to their faded glory. "Your father's family," he had written in 1825, "cannot get clear of the notion of what they once were." His future, he told Bo, did not lie in being joined to a family whose fortunes were rapidly diminishing in a society based on idleness; it lay in America, where a young man with a good education but modest means "may rise to consequence."

In offering this advice to his grandson, William left the obvious unsaid: his own daughter shared the Bonapartes' illusions. But marriage to an American heiress—this would be an excellent step in a young man's "rise to consequence." The tug-of-war over Bo's future, long waged between Betsy and her father, was about to end in triumph for William Patterson, and he intended to assist Bo's courtship of Susan in any way he could.

The only stumbling block to the marriage was money. Susan was the heir to a huge fortune left by her father, but her mother was initially wary of a suitor with few resources of his own. To help the courtship along, William Patterson assured Mrs. Williams that he would provide Bo with a generous portion of his own wealth, including several valuable Baltimore properties and a cash settlement that, in modern currency, would equal almost half a million dollars. This promise dispelled all doubts, and in turn the widow Williams pledged that her future son-in-law would have the authority to manage the family fortune. The annual income from that fortune, some $8,000, would be his to enjoy as he saw fit. This arrangement gave Bo thousands of dollars more than Betsy's investments provided her each year. And Bo could spend this money as he chose, without fear of hearing a lecture from his parsimonious mother.

Everyone who knew of the arrangement seemed satisfied. But Betsy was not aware that an arrangement had been made. In July 1829, William had written to her only that Bo was courting a young woman and that, as the young man's grandfather, William had consented to the match. Bo had acted judiciously, William assured his daughter; he had always been "determined not to marry unless he met with one with such a fortune as would make him independent through life," and Susan May Williams could do just that. "You will no doubt be greatly surprised at this determination of your sons [*sic*], but I trust & expect that you will on mature reflection see that it is a wise & rational measure & the very best that could be hoped for or expected in his situation." The implied criticism of Betsy—that she could not provide her son with the wealth needed to lead an independent life—and the triumphant tone of the entire letter surely struck home.

Still Betsy was kept carefully in the dark about how far along the courtship had progressed. Thus, while William Patterson was arranging the financial settlement that would make her son a wealthy man, Betsy was busily mapping out other plans for his future. Perhaps a diplomatic career would suit him. Perhaps William and her uncle, Samuel Smith, could talk to President Andrew Jackson about naming Bo secretary to the legation at the embassy in London. She would somehow find the money to support him there in appropriate style. These plans revived her dream that Bo might marry into a titled family, perhaps by taking as a bride a Galitzin or Potemkin or Demidov princess.

All of Betsy's "perhaps"es hinged on aborting Bo's courtship of an American woman. She sent her father a letter in September, urging that Bo abandon his pursuit of a Baltimore bride. He must be told that she would never give her consent to a marriage to Miss Williams or to any American woman. In her desperation, she declared that she would act in a manner reminiscent of Napoleon twenty-six years before: "If he were a Minor I would go to America & avail myself of the Laws of the country to prevent or dissolve the mean marriage." A few weeks later she wrote again, this time softening her tone and rescinding her threat. "I am sorry," she told William, "that in the first shock I felt when I read your & his letter I was hurried into the expression of feelings which may have appeared extraordinary to you." Despite the conciliatory tone, Betsy's sense of helplessness in the face of what she suspected was a conspiracy to destroy her dreams prompted her to add: "If this marriage should have been hurried on to prevent my interference, for I feel persuaded that everyone of them know that I have too much sense & too much pride ever to give my consent I will then declare in the face of the whole world that I utterly disclaim all participation in it."

Betsy's suspicions were sadly correct. Her brother Edward confessed to her that both Bo and William had taken pains to hide the progress of the courtship from her. On November 3, 1829, the very day she was told that her son was engaged, Bo and Susan were married. William's letter carrying the news, written the day after the ceremony was performed, made it clear that her efforts to prevent it had come too late. If fortune had at last smiled on Bo, it had laughed once more at Elizabeth Patterson Bonaparte.

Betsy's rage was palpable, but as usual, William had no sympathy for his daughter's distress. Had Bo dashed her hopes and dreams? Had he acted in direct contradiction to her wishes? She had no right to complain, he wrote, for her own disobedience and her own rejection of her family's expectations had been far more extreme. William urged her to "look back on your own conduct in relinquishing your family and country for an imaginary consequence amongst strangers who care little for you. . . . Indeed," he continued, "rather than being displeased with your son's late conduct you ought to commend him for his prudence and forethought in providing so well for his future prospects."

Betsy could not immediately reply to this barrage of blame and accusation. Finally, in a December 4 letter to William, she wrote, "I think that I did my duty in trying to elevate his ideas above marrying in America." But it had all been for naught. "He has neither my pride, my ambition, nor my love of good company, therefore I no longer oppose his marriage."

What surely ate at Betsy's soul was that William's values and William's tastes had triumphed over her own. Her son, like her father, embraced American culture, from its hearty and simple cuisine to its creation of an aristocracy based on wealth rather than bloodline. And in Susan May Williams, Bo had chosen a woman far more like his grandmother Dorcas Spear Patterson than his mother, a woman who did not charm with sparkling wit or dazzle with brilliant observations on politics and literature. Like William's wife, Susan would ensure Bo a perfect blending of two necessities in his life: wealth and unchallenged patriarchal authority.

A letter from Bo did little to cool her anger. Her son begged her to understand his motives. "Please Understand, Maman," he wrote, "that in my future life I can never get along without money. Yet as you know, the allowance from my father is precarious, and grandfather has not, so far, promised to do anything for me. Contrary to your wishes, I have no desire to follow a diplomatic career. Business is what I like, and for that I need something to fall back on." Bo's explanation was carefully crafted. William Patterson had, of course, provided amply for his grandson in the marriage negotiations; perhaps Bo hoped to exaggerate his plight, gambling that his mother did not know of the large marriage settlement. It was an artful ploy, worthy of his own father. One thing is clear: with this letter, Bo at last told Betsy bluntly who he was and what he desired in life.

Those who knew Bo well were not surprised by his actions. Even William, who loved Bo deeply, recognized that his grandson lacked the qualities that defined a self-made man. Bo was "by nature rather indolent and without much ambition" and thus had chosen a path that suited his character. Betsy's brother Edward had also taken his nephew's measure over the years and wrote that the marriage was, as Bo himself conceded to his mother, "a mercenary transaction altogether and carried through in a purely mercantile spirit." And where was the surprise in that? Edward asked. What else was to be expected when there was "a total want of ambition in Jerome and an inordinate desire of wealth on his part"?

It was, of course, Betsy, not Bo, who shared William's pride in being self-made, in succeeding through her own efforts. But she had not seen what both her father and her brother had seen in Bo's character. She had always viewed her son through the halo glow of her own hopes and dreams for an only child. She had planned meticulously, fervently, for his future without a clear picture of his inclinations, his interests, or his abilities. Now, rather than accepting Bo as he was, she nurtured an intense sense of betrayal.

On December 21 she dropped all pretense that she was reconciled to events. She would never condone the marriage, she told her father. She would not disown Bo, as she believed William had disowned her—he was her legitimate heir, and she would do her duty as his mother. But she would no longer sacrifice for her son. She would spend all the funds that her investments spun off each year on herself. "I have gained my fortune by the strictest economy—by privations of every kind," she declared, and she would not see the fruits of her labor go to "strangers" like Susan Williams. Her anger, her sense of betrayal by an ungrateful son, was a distant, ironic echo of Napoleon Bonaparte's reaction to her marriage to his favorite brother.

Disturbing as Bo's marriage was, it was not the only surprising event that 1829 would bring to the life of Elizabeth Patterson Bonaparte. For in the same year that Bo married for money, his mother fell in love. At forty-four, despite all her protestations that love was sheer foolishness, out of fashion even among novelists and poets, Betsy began a romance with a young Russian named Prince Alexander Mikhailovich Gorchakov.

Prince Gorchakov was a thirty-one-year-old attaché at the Russian embassy in Florence. He was blond and handsome, with a high forehead and eyes that revealed a deep and probing intelligence. He would rise to be the chancellor of the Russian Empire under Tsar Alexander II, but in the 1820s his career was just beginning. He shared with Betsy a disdain for insipid gossip and a love of serious conversation. He also shared with her a tendency to hide his more serious nature from others, to take on a flirtatious persona that charmed but kept those he charmed at arm's length. Betsy quickly recognized in him the same depths she knew to exist in herself. "A duller person," she told him, "could not have seen through the mist with which your caprice and impertinence envelope you."

Betsy's attraction to Gorchakov shone through in the undated description of him she kept for the rest of her life: it spoke of his "unique simplicity," his "generous sentiments," and his exquisite taste. Yet Betsy knew his faults as well as his virtues: he was intensely ambitious and vain, two qualities that defined her as precisely as they did the prince. And just as Betsy enjoyed being courted by men, Gorchakov was a man who wished all women to adore him, even if he felt no love for them in return. To win his love, Betsy declared, a woman "must be beautiful, spirited," and she must be in demand and fashionable and be considered as charming by others as by himself. This portrait of Gorchakov's ideal woman fit Betsy perfectly.

So many men had courted Betsy over the decades, but none had stirred her emotions as Gorchakov did. In Alexander she had found a man not only as charming as she, but as intelligent. For months, the pair engaged in spirited arguments about philosophy, politics, and poetry. Often their discussions collapsed into heated argument, for he was as stubbornly confident of his views as she was of hers. When they were not debating the merits of a poem or a philosophical principle, they challenged each other in contests of wit and penned word portraits of friends and enemies.

Watching Alexander and Betsy, their Russian friends knew they were witnessing the sparring of brilliant equals and the electricity of a doomed attraction. It was clear to all that the relationship would not, could not, end in marriage, for Alexander had to marry a woman of the Russian aristocracy if he hoped to fulfill his ambitions as a national leader.

Alexander's solution to their dilemma was as simple as it was acceptable to the society in which they traveled: Betsy must become his mistress. But Betsy refused. Like Caesar's wife, she had taken care, since her marriage to Jérôme ended, to lead a life above reproach. No matter how tempted she was now, she would do nothing that might cast doubt on her moral character. She guarded her honor carefully, for to do otherwise would suggest that Napoleon had annulled her marriage on moral grounds. For Betsy's pride, and for her son's reputation, the annulment must stand as a purely political decision. Thus through all the years since Jérôme abandoned her, despite all the suitors, all the men who longed to bed her or to marry her, none, not even Alexander Gorchakov, would succeed.

Chapter Thirteen

"Disgusted with the Past, Despairing of a Future"

I n 1834 Betsy left Europe. Her romance with Alexander Gorchakov was long over, and the charms of the continent had paled. A cholera epidemic, begun in 1826, still raged, taking thousands upon thousands of lives. Many of her friends had fled to the countryside, leaving Paris, Rome, and Florence in hopes of avoiding the gruesome death that reminded many of the bubonic plague. The political and social face of Europe was, in Betsy's view, equally blighted. The July Revolution of 1830 had created a constitutional monarchy in France, and the new king, Louis-Philippe, now ruled as "King of the French" rather than as the French king. The implication was clear: France's citizens were sovereign, and the king they put on the throne must rule in their best interest. The revolution in France sparked revolutions in the Netherlands, Belgium, and Poland. Cholera was thus not the only epidemic sweeping across the continent; democracy was threatening to make bloodlines less important in Europe than the ability to amass wealth.

In America, William Patterson had watched the turmoil produced by these events with concern—and a measure of satisfaction at the crumbling of the world his daughter had so admired. "Every thing is turning upside down in Europe," he wrote as the

July Revolution's impact began to be felt across that continent, and there would be "confusion & distress . . . before things can settle down in any regular way." He predicted, "It is not likely there will be a crowned head left except at the will of the people," for "they are all looking forward to independence & Republicanism & nothing short of this will satisfy them." He clearly felt that Europe was becoming more American every day.

Betsy's response to the declining power of Europe's aristocrats was a measure of how consumed with bitterness and anger she had become in the wake of Bo's marriage and the loss of Alexander. In her darkest mood, she proclaimed her hope that the aristocratic classes would at last experience the suffering she had long endured. "Let them all descend from their rank & try the disgusting life as citizens," she wrote to her friend and financial manager, John White. Why should they escape the "blighted existence" she had endured? The weariness that this attack on the aristocrats who had befriended her conveyed was no romantic posturing; in 1834 she felt "old, enfeebled by misery of every sort, soured by disappointments, disgusted with the Past, despairing of a future which can afford me nothing."

In America, a different plague seemed to be spreading, and the entire national economy appeared to be in chaos. The nation's president, Andrew Jackson, had done battle with the Bank of the United States and had won: he vetoed the renewal of a charter for this financial institution, created by Alexander Hamilton in the 1790s. But in slaying what he called the dragon of economic privilege, he unleashed economic instability, panic, and depression. William Patterson used the economic crisis as an occasion to reprimand his daughter. "We are in great confusion and distress in this country," he told her, adding that "there is no saying how it may end, or that it may not ultimately bring about a revolution. Your presence here is absolutely necessary to look after your affairs and property, and the sooner the better." For once, Betsy decided her father was right.

The America she was returning to had, like Europe, experienced a surge of democratic reform. In a land whose credo was now more solidly egalitarian and whose feminine ideal was more firmly domestic, Betsy's aristocratic tastes would continue to alienate neighbors and family. She knew she had no choice but to return to Baltimore and manage her property there, yet she could not accept now, any more than she could in the past, her father's conviction that "sweet home and the natural intercourse and connexion with our family is, after all, the only chance for happiness in this world."

By 1834, Betsy had felt the winds of change on both continents. But perhaps the change that shook her most deeply was an intimate one: her father had grown old. In a letter in August 1833, Nancy Spear had warned Betsy what to expect: "Your Father is excessively old & miserably infirm." But the shock of seeing the man who had so dominated her life for what he now was—lonely and feeble—must have been great. A decade before, the Patterson patriarch had found himself in a house empty except for a mistress. To remedy his loneliness, he had brought his son Henry to live with him. But it was his attachment to Betsy, expressed as always in a potent mix of criticism and disapproval, that remained his most intense emotional con-

nection. Now in old age, he revealed to Nancy Spear the longing that lay beneath the surface of that criticism. "He frequently
talks of you to me & of your leaving him," she told Betsy. It was
time, she continued, to heal the breach. "I wish most ardently
you would forgive him for your own sake as well as his, for he
is almost childish."

William's recent letters to his daughter revealed the twisted
expression of this need. "How could you have neglected the duty
of writing for so long a time," he wrote in perverse welcome to
the news that his daughter was returning home. This reprimand
was followed by the surprising confession that "it still affords
me much pleasure to have heard from you at length."

Betsy's relationship with her father was not the only emotional Gordian knot she faced. She had not seen her only child
since they said their goodbyes in 1825. Now in 1834, Bo was not
only a husband but also the father of a four-year-old boy. Betsy
could not forgive his marriage, and she could not accept Susan
May Williams into her family, yet she found herself drawn to
her grandson, the third male in her life to carry the name Jerome
Bonaparte. As this Jerome grew older, he would find many of
her old dreams of greatness rewoven around him as they had
once been woven around his father.

In the winter of 1835, the long war—and its brief, fragile
truce—between Betsy and her father at last ended. William Patterson died that February, leaving behind a will that testified to
his enduring anger at a daughter who would not accede to his
wishes, heed his advice, or lead a life he could approve. When
the will was published in the local newspaper, his condemnation

of Betsy became a matter of public record. Despite his promise in her marriage contract of 1803, she would not receive an equal share of his estate. "The conduct of my daughter Betsey has through life been so disobedient that in no instance has she ever consulted my opinions or feelings; indeed, she has caused me more anxiety and trouble than all my other children put together, and her folly and misconduct have occasioned me a train of expense that first and last has cost me much money. Under such circumstances it would not be reasonable, just, or proper that she should inherit and participate in an equal proportion with my other children in an equal division of my estate." Insult was then added to injury, for William announced a willingness to temper justice with mercy: "Considering, however, the weakness of human nature, and that she is still my daughter," he had chosen not to entirely exclude her from a share in his property.

Had William failed to revise his will in that last year, when Betsy had come home to him? Would he have removed its condemnation and punishment had death not come upon him so soon after his daughter's return? No one will ever know. But Betsy's resentment and hurt could still be felt years later when she wrote: "The clause in his will which relates to myself plainly betrays the embarrassment of a loaded conscience, & of a bad cause." Her anger was as enduring as his, her condemnation as complete: "He had violated every principle of honour & of equity to make a ruin of my ambition, of my hopes & of my happiness. & it has ever been a principle in human nature that men cannot forgive those to whom they have been guilty of

great cruelty, perfidy & injustice." In her mind, William's ani-
mosity toward her was a companion sin to his contemptuous
infidelity to her mother: "The grave of my Mother had never
interposed a barrier between herself & this malignant & relentless hatred with which he had pursued her from the day of her
fatal marriage to him." With this will, he had meted out his
vengeance from the grave, hoping to drown Betsy's defense of
herself—not as he had done with his wife, through a demand
for feminine submission, but with his "falsehood, persecution,
injustice & calumny." Still, Betsy felt a sense of triumph, for,
in their battle of wills, she had always been his equal. "He had
flattered himself," she wrote, "that his firmness of purpose & his
cunning could defraud Death of the right to freeze that torrent
of injuries & of misfortunes of which he my father had been to
me the first, the copious & the unfailing Source," yet he had
defeated neither death nor Elizabeth Patterson Bonaparte.

Betsy may have privately shed tears over the loss of her father.
She surely shed them over the humiliation he had meted out
to her. But tears would not wash away the injustice she had
suffered. To do that, she must contest the will, and this, she
knew, would require that she take legal action. She went looking for a lawyer. In the end, she decided on not one but three:
two who represented one of Philadelphia's premier firms dealing
with contested wills, and one, Roger B. Taney, who was about
to become the chief justice of the U.S. Supreme Court.

Betsy did not go to these men as a helpless female, eager to
place her fate in their more capable hands. She came to them
prepared with the materials she believed they would need to

win her an equal share of William's estate. She brought the 1803 marriage agreement that her father had signed, with its promise that she would receive a share equal to her siblings' of her father's property. She alerted them to her mother's verbal deathbed will, which bequeathed funds to Betsy and which her father had ignored. She composed a list of questions for each of them, hoping to guide the direction of their arguments. This preparation focused on the past; the present proved more complicated.

At William's death, six of his children remained living, Betsy and five of her brothers. One of these men, John Patterson, had as much reason to be as indignant as Betsy, for he was scarcely mentioned in his father's will. William had given John property in Virginia several decades before and apparently felt his parental obligation to this son had been fulfilled. All John could now expect was some household furnishings—and a fifth share of William's wine cellar. Joseph, Edward, George, and Henry, on the other hand, received city real estate, businesses, warehouses, and wharves, shares in their father's ships, and bank and other company stock. They were heirs as well to William's country estates and to the slaves who labored there. Betsy's own son, Bo, had been generously provided for through bank stock, Baltimore real estate, and one of the country estates, Pleasant View.

Bo, always ready to enjoy wealth that he did not earn himself, resented that his share of William's estate was smaller than his uncles'. His dissatisfaction made him Betsy's firm ally in her efforts to challenge the will. For as his mother's direct heir, Bo had a stake in the outcome of her lawsuit. His marriage to Susan

May Williams had driven a wedge between mother and son; his eagerness to secure future wealth now united them.

The biggest hurdle facing mother and son was the penalty clause William had inserted in his will. Hoping no doubt to prevent the very actions Betsy had now set in motion, William wrote: "Should any of my heirs be so far dissatisfied and unreasonable as to attempt to break and undo this my Will," that person would forfeit everything. To ensure that the remaining heirs would not provide support to the challenger, William declared that the forfeited property would be divided equally among his more obedient legatees.

Was the penalty clause enforceable? Betsy's lawyers assured her it was not. Was William Patterson of "sound mind" when the will was signed? They thought not. The distribution of the estate, they declared, was so arbitrary, the document itself so unusual, that they suspected it was the work of a deranged mind. And yet . . . they conceded that a challenge to the will would be unlikely to succeed. The 1803 wedding contract, on the other hand, was just that, a contract, and it could be enforced. The problem was that Betsy and Bo could not expect to collect what was promised to them in the marriage contract *and* what was bequeathed to them in the will. They had to choose one or the other. Determining which was more advantageous was no simple task, however. Myriad questions remained unanswered: What, exactly, was the value of each of the properties William owned? What was the value of the stocks and bank shares? Were the properties and stocks bequeathed to Betsy and Bo worth more than the one-third of his 1803 estate promised to her in the marriage contract? The best course of action, the lawyers concluded, was to petition the court of equity for a complete accounting of the entire estate and its value.

Unfortunately, pursuing this best course of action would make it impossible for Betsy or Bo to touch the property and wealth granted to them by the will until the accounting process was finished. This dilemma spawned a new dilemma: If the two did not work in tandem, what would be the consequences? If, for instance, Bo decided to file in the court of equity but Betsy chose to accept the terms of the will, what would be the legal consequences?

Whatever decisions she and Bo made, they would not be made in a vacuum. While her lawyers were busy drafting their opinions, her brothers were busy mounting a counteroffensive.

They had found William's copy of the marriage contract and had enlisted Nancy Spear, long Betsy's confidante and one of her financial advisers, to discover if Betsy too had a copy of the contract. If she did not, they had every intention of keeping her in the dark about the copy they had discovered. Betsy was no fool, however; she quickly realized what they were up to—and refused to reveal that she not only had a copy but had shared it with her lawyers. The brothers then tried a new tack. Perhaps they could find evidence in Betsy's correspondence that would justify William's depiction of her as a willful, troublesome, and undeserving child. Once again they turned to Nancy Spear, who proved more than eager to help out: she sold all the letters that Betsy had written her to Joseph and Edward.

Betsy was more hurt than frightened by the attempt to use

her letters as a weapon against her. She had saved Nancy's letters too, after all, and among them was a "graphic description, written by her, of the Introduction and expulsion of Matilda Somers," William Patterson's illegitimate child by one of his many mistresses. She warned her brothers that she would make this letter public if they attempted to use any of her correspondence against her.

The matter ended here, but its consequences were felt for years to come. The close relationship between Edward Patterson and Betsy was shattered, for he had been a party to the purchase of her letters. "Edward loved me," Betsy wrote, "until the bad old man's will killed his affection." As for Joseph, there could be no reconciliation. He and Edward had "menaced" her with the publication of her letters. A new distance also developed between Betsy and her brother George, who had earlier won her respect by turning over his share of their mother's property to Betsy. But he had refused to support her in the controversy over William's estate. And Betsy and Nancy Spear never spoke again. In a letter to George, Betsy explained why there could be no reconciliation. "Having told many Persons that the Will was perfectly, admirably just," Nancy had forfeited her claim on Betsy's friendship. "Respectful Neutrality & Becoming silence on her part, were imperiously commanded by Good Sense (in Default of Gratitude) for the long continued & innumerable obligations, which the world has, with perfect truth, considered her to lie under to me." Soon after, in a scathing poem, Betsy poured out her feelings about her friend's betrayal, condemning her "Quaint Companion, / Whose viper tongue did ever gore /

The friendly hand it fed on." Long after Nancy's death in 1836, that betrayal still burned brightly in Betsy's memory.

Perhaps most painful to Betsy, however, was the toll that the long, drawn-out legal process took on her relationship with Bo. Their alliance had held the promise of rapprochement between mother and son, but as the matter dragged on, an icy formality on Bo's part returned. Her son continued to send her reports from meetings with the Philadelphia lawyers, yet as Betsy sadly noted, "He never says 'Dear Mama' any more. He doesn't end with anything."

In the end, Betsy abandoned her legal struggle. She accepted the terms of her father's will, acknowledging that, with careful management, she would have enough income to live comfortably for the rest of her life. But where she would live out that life remained uncertain. Her distaste for Baltimore and the loss of her small circle of friends like Edward and Nancy Spear made her long to escape once again to Europe. She had once written that "no one who has lived long in Europe can ever be happy out of it." Happiness, she conceded, might not be possible anywhere, but in France or Switzerland or Italy "there are more ways . . . of forgetting one's misfortunes than can be found in America." By the summer of 1839, the wish to forget her misfortunes prompted Betsy to set sail across the Atlantic once again.

Chapter Fourteen

"My Birth Is Legitimate"

B etsy went to Paris to forget her misfortunes, but this time Europe proved no antidote. Here, in the City of Light, she felt the same weariness that had burdened her in Baltimore, and she feared that "melancholy and regrets have become a chronic disease from which I can never recover." Writing to her friend Sydney Morgan, she admitted that her two months in Paris had "passed very dully," for "death, time and absence have left me scarcely an acquaintance at Paris." Friends like David Warden who did remain had grown old. He was, she told Sydney, "unchanged in kind feelings, but, poor man, time has dealt hard with his exterior; he looks as if he had begun to exist a century ago." In this respect, Warden was not alone; Betsy believed that she too had been worn down by time. She was fifty-five, and she had, she told Sydney, "grown fat, old and dull, all good reasons for people not to think me an intelligent hearer or listener."

Bo too had come to Europe, but not to escape his life in Baltimore—he was headed to Italy to see the Bonapartes. It was far from a social visit: despite all the extravagant promises his father's family had once made to Betsy and her son, little fortune had come to him from them. But Cardinal Fesch, Madame Mère's brother, had not forgotten him. On his death, the cardinal had left his grandnephew a small legacy, and Bo now hurried to collect it. Betsy no doubt envied her son, for she too would have preferred to make Italy her destination. If she could live anywhere, she told Sydney, it would be Florence. But this was not possible, for "there lives there one individual whom I wish not to meet again." She no longer cared if Jérôme had been the willing or the "unreflecting cause" of spoiling what she still considered her true destiny—a lawful place within the Bonaparte family during Napoleon's reign—but she wished to avoid any possibility of encountering her former husband. There was nothing for her to do, she knew, but go home once again.

Home, for Betsy, might have meant Baltimore, but it did not mean the house in which she had grown up, even though William had bequeathed it to her. She had spent much of her adult life in boardinghouses, rented apartments, and guest quarters in other peoples' homes and villas. She had never set up house-keeping herself, and she had felt no desire to do so now. Instead, she moved into a boardinghouse on Lexington Street.

Here her life took on a pattern: she spent her summers at Rockaway Beach, a resort near New York City frequented by European diplomats and sophisticated urban dwellers eager to escape the heat; she spent winters in Baltimore; and she made an occasional visit to a spa in Virginia. Her companion on many of her summers at the beach was her grandson. Although Betsy never warmed to his "unamiable mother," she doted on the young Bonaparte whom the family called "Junior."

Then in 1848, with a suddenness that jolted Betsy, everything changed. News came from Europe that King Louis-Philippe's government had failed and a French republic had been declared. Miraculously, Bo's cousin, Louis-Napoleon, whose reckless attempts to bring down the king and establish himself as the emperor had landed him in prison in the late 1830s, had been elected France's new president. The news thrilled Betsy; she saw Louis-Napoleon's ascent to power as an act of homage to the memory of Napoleon Bonaparte himself. Writing to Sydney Morgan, she confessed, "I do feel enchanted at the homage paid by six millions of voices to [Napoleon's] memory in voting an imperial president." Democracy, which she had long abhorred, seemed vindicated by the wisdom French voters had shown. "I never could endure universal suffrage until it elected the nephew of an emperor for the chief of a republic," she declared, "and I shall be charmed with universal suffrage once more if it insists upon their president of France becoming a monarch."

The developments in Europe prompted the resurgence of Betsy's old hatred of life in Baltimore. When Sydney wrote to her that she and her husband had moved to London, Betsy decided to pack her bags once again. She had no desire, she said, to go to France, for her former husband and his family had joined other Bonapartes in Paris. But she would gladly go to London. When the sad news arrived that Sydney Morgan's husband had suddenly died, Betsy knew she must hurry to console her friend. Although she was nearing her sixty-fifth birthday, Betsy once again crossed the Atlantic. Before the year was out, she was in England.

While Betsy and Sydney passed their days taking drives and talking over dinner, Louis-Napoleon was busy proving that his ambition was equal to that of his famous uncle. The "prince-president," as he liked to call himself, faced one major hurdle in his plans to establish a regime reminiscent of Napoleon's: the new constitution did not allow a president to run for reelection. To get around this, he staged a coup d'état, and with the aid of the army and the mass arrests of his opponents, he succeeded in extending his authority beyond the end of his presidential term. By December 1852, he was powerful enough to establish the Second Empire. No longer simply "prince-president," he was now known as the emperor Napoleon III. His dreams—and Betsy's hopes—had come true.

Betsy's hopes no longer centered on her son but on her grandson. After she returned to Baltimore in 1850, she followed events in France carefully. She was convinced, by the spring of 1852, even before Louis-Napoleon became emperor, that Junior ought to cast his lot with his father's cousin. Writing to James Gallatin that May, she lamented, "I only wish that my Grand Son could be at Paris." By November of that year, she was still expressing regret that Junior had not made his way to the French capital. "My Grand Son remains in this Country, which is not my fault you may very certainly believe." But by now she was accustomed to him ignoring her advice; all she could do was remind her friends that it was not her fault if her family members were less ambitious, less politically astute than their aging mother and grandmother.

Betsy made no effort to hide her ambition for Junior from her friends and family. But when strangers like the editors of *The New American Cyclopaedia* publicly alleged that she had prophesied that her grandson would become the third to rule as a French emperor, she quickly wrote a rebuttal. "I have never coveted for one I so much love as I do my Grand Son a crown," she declared, adding, "Had I been capable of such folly, I, at least, possess sufficient American acuteness never to have by prophecies given verbal utterance to it. The inference to be drawn from what you have published on this subject, is that I am either demented or imbecile; of this I do not complain, but I do of an unfounded assertion which might prove injurious to my grandson." Betsy's motive was obvious: she did not want the emperor to think she was plotting his replacement or challenging his abilities to rule. She demanded that the editors "nullify what you have erroneously, & not, I am willing to believe, from the malignant suggestion of others, stated in the paragraph respecting prophecies."

Less quickly than Betsy might have wished, Bo sent his cousin a letter of congratulations. He was genuinely fond of Louis-Napoleon, whom he had met in Rome when they were both young. The friendship had been renewed, briefly, when Louis visited in Baltimore in 1837. King Louis-Philippe had sent the troublemaking Louis away from France that year, but Louis-Napoleon wasted little time getting a fake passport so that he could return to Europe to plot and plan once more. Now in 1853 the new emperor replied to his cousin in America that he had "received with great pleasure the letter which conveys to me your congratulations and good wishes," adding, "When circumstances permit, believe me, I shall be very happy to see you again."

Bo took the emperor's words as an invitation. The following year he and his son, now a graduate of West Point, traveled to Paris. Susan Bonaparte remained at home with a new son, born twenty years after Junior, named Charles. The emperor greeted his American relatives warmly, inviting them to dinner at his palace at Saint-Cloud. Here he presented Bo with a paper on which the minister of justice, the president of the French Senate, and the president of the Council of State recorded their opinion that the marriage of Prince Jérôme and Elizabeth Patterson was legitimate—and thus that Jerome Napoleon Bonaparte of Baltimore, Maryland, was a legitimate child of France. A decree by the emperor could restore French citizenship to Bo, if Bo wished. And as the offer might have financial benefits, Bo did.

More signs of favor followed. Empress Eugénie was so impressed by Junior that her husband urged the West Point graduate to consider a career in the French army. By the summer of 1854, Junior had resigned his commission in the U.S. Army and begun his career as a second lieutenant in the Seventh Regiment of Dragoons. Soon afterward he headed to the Crimea to join the allied armies of Turkey, Great Britain, and France in their war with Russia. Here his bravery on the battlefield won the admiration of French officers and earned him several citations for bravery and a promotion to first lieutenant.

At first this reunion of the American and French branches of the Bonaparte family seemed to please all the family members. But tensions soon developed between Bo and his father's family, who were firmly ensconced in Paris. Jérôme, now the former king of Westphalia, had settled here as Louis-Napoleon's star had risen. The emperor had generously provided his uncle with a government post that required him to do little and paid well. He also invited Jérôme and his family—which now consisted of a mistress Jérôme had elevated to wife after Catherine's death, his daughter Princess Mathilde, and his one surviving son with Catherine, Prince Napoleon—to take up residence at the Palais Royale. Prince Napoleon had quickly established himself in French politics, taking an active role in the General Assembly. To the emperor's dismay, the young politician was known for his criticism of Louis-Napoleon's policies. The prince was ambitious and competitive—and far from likable. A Parisian who knew him well described him as "the most prodigiously intelligent and prodigiously vicious man that ever lived."

This vicious prince quickly grew jealous of Junior's battlefield successes. His own military career had been less than stellar. He had been appointed to a generalship in the French army but saw little action during the Crimean War. In fact, he withdrew from active service, claiming illness. The soldiers serving under him told a very different story about his withdrawal from the battlefield. They said he was so frightened by the *plomb plomb* of the cannons that he fled to the safety of Paris. Their nickname for the erstwhile general reflected their contempt: to them, he was not Napoleon but "Plon Plon." If Plon Plon chafed at his nephew's medals and commendations, he was even more disturbed by the emperor's generosity toward Bo. Louis-Napoleon had offered Bo an impressive pension of 70,000 francs a year and announced his intention to make him the Duke of Sartène and Junior the Count of Sartène.

At issue was far more than a competition for the emperor's affections. In 1852 the then-childless emperor had established an order of succession that greatly favored Plon Plon. "In the event that we should leave no direct heir of legitimate birth or adopted," Napoleon III had written, "our well-beloved uncle, Jérôme Napoleon Bonaparte, and his direct legitimate descendants resulting from his marriage with the Princess Catherine of Württemberg, from male to male, in the order of primogeniture, and to the exclusion of females, shall be called upon to succeed us." Napoleon III then had a son, born in March 1856, but Plon Plon was eager to ensure that no American Bonaparte challenged his place in the line of succession. Soon enough Betsy's ex-husband was enlisted to pressure Napoleon III to reconsider his generosity toward his American wife and her family. "Your decrees," he wrote the emperor, "dispose of my name without my consent. They introduce into my family, without my having ever been consulted, persons who have never formed any part of it." Jérôme went so far as to declare the recognition of his son Bo as "an attack upon my honor."

Bo soon realized that he was caught up in the byzantine politics so common to the Bonaparte family. He began to suspect that the emperor might be using him as a pawn to pressure Plon Plon to soften his criticism of imperial policy. He grew even more suspicious of his role in this family drama when Louis-Napoleon made it a quid pro quo that he give up the name Bonaparte in exchange for the title of Duke of Sartène.

Bo's pride made such an exchange impossible. His resentment increased when his son was offered a knighthood in the

French Legion of Honor, but the notification was addressed to "Lt. Jerome Bonaparte-Patterson." Junior returned the letter, noting that it was "addressed to him under a name which was not his own."

Soon enough, the core issue emerged fully: Was Bo a legitimate candidate for the throne? Plon Plon and his grandfather, the former king of Württemberg, were determined to establish that he was not. They demanded that the emperor call a Council of the Family to decide whether Jerome Patterson of Maryland and his descendants were entitled to bear the Bonaparte name.

In the decision they handed down on July 4, 1856, the council finessed the question. Its members—the emperor, a prince of the family, the minister of state, the minister of justice, the president of the Senate and of the Assembly, a member of the Council of State, a marshal of France, and a member of the nation's highest court—ruled that while Betsy's marriage to Jérôme had been nullified under Napoleon I, the surname Bonaparte could not be taken away from Bo or his descendants. The larger victory, however, went to Plon Plon: the council also ruled that Bo had no rights under Articles 201 and 202 of the Civil Code to inherit from his father. In other words, Bo was a bastard child. As the emperor put it in a note he attached to the council decree, Bo and his descendants were not to be considered "as belonging to his *famille civile*." With that, the American branch of the Bonaparte family was excluded from the succession.

Bo responded to the decision with dignity. Writing to the emperor on July 28, he again declined the titles and honors that had been offered to him and to his son and declared: "Since no man creates himself, there is no dishonor to be born a bastard and to accept the consequences. Had I been in that category, I would have long ago accepted, and with gratitude, the offers which Your Majesty has deigned to make me. But, since my birth is legitimate and has always been so recognized by my family, by the laws of all countries and by the whole world, it would be the height of cowardice and of dishonor to accept a warrant of bastardy." With that, Bo requested the emperor's permission to "go with his son into exile and await there the justice that, I am sure, heaven will reserve for me, sooner or later."

Bo had retreated, but he had not surrendered entirely. He knew that, with his father's death, an opportunity to reassert his membership in the *famille civile* would arise.

Before leaving France, therefore, he contacted one of that nation's most famous lawyers, Pierre-Antoine Berryer, the very man who had defended Louis-Napoleon against King Louis-Philippe's charge of high treason in the 1830s. He gave Berryer power of attorney and provided him with documents relevant to the case. He promised to send more supporting materials when he arrived in America. Clearly, the battle over Bo's legitimacy was not over.

Betsy was cruelly disappointed by the rise and sudden fall of the American Bonapartes in Paris. She followed the unfolding of events in the newspapers, for coverage of the warm reception and then the rejection of Bo and his son appeared in papers from New York to Savannah to Newark, Ohio. Her only consolation was that her grandson did not return to Baltimore with his father but remained an officer in the French army. Whatever her hopes were for him now, she wanted to ensure that he would cut an appropriately aristocratic figure in European society. Over the next several years, she sent him large sums of money for his horses, his military uniforms, and his housing in Paris.

Despite the seeming finality of the council's ruling, Betsy, like Bo, believed the battle with Plon Plon and his father was not over. In 1858 she began sending the lawyer Berryer documents she thought might be useful, including those relating to her Maryland divorce. And like Bo, she gave Berryer power of attorney to act on her behalf. She intended, she told the lawyer, "to ascertain, vindicate, and enforce my rights." Over the next few years, she rehearsed her past again and again, in letters to Berryer and in letters to friends, like those both sent and unsent to Prince Gorchakov.

Then on June 24, 1860, Betsy's former husband, Jérôme Bonaparte, died at the age of seventy-six. Newspapers across America carried the news, sometimes reviewing the history of the European Bonaparte family, but more often retelling the story of Elizabeth Patterson Bonaparte's ill-fated marriage. In this manner, Betsy's celebrity was revived. Sympathy for Jérôme was scarce in the columns of American newspapers. "His death creates no vacuum in public affairs," noted the Milwaukee *Daily Sentinel,* "for his life has never been the hinge of great events." But the story of a beautiful American woman, abandoned by a weak-willed husband and sacrificed to the ambitions of a foreign emperor, inspired the newspaper reporters. "His first wife," a typical article noted, "still resides in Baltimore, and through a life that is now long, has remained faithful to her first and only marriage vows, whose annulment she would never acknowledge, while her faithless and weak husband . . . has forgotten both his first and last, and dying, bears no nobler title than the last of the family of the Corsican."

Only a month before Americans learned of Jérôme's death, the Republican Party had nominated Abraham Lincoln to be president, and the United States moved closer to a civil war. The American Bonapartes, too, began to prepare for a war, not over slavery or secession but over legitimacy and succession. This struggle would be followed closely in newspapers at home and abroad.

Chapter Fifteen

"I Will Never Be Dupe Enough Ever to Try Justice in France"

F ort Sumter had been fired on; an American civil war had indeed begun. But *Harper's Weekly* found room on its pages in early 1861 for a picture of Betsy and an article about her life and marriage. The impending court case in France, like news of Jérôme's death, had revived national interest in Elizabeth Patterson Bonaparte and her son's claim to legitimacy. In newspapers across the country, the story of the Patterson-Bonaparte marriage was again retold.

By the time the *Harper's Weekly* story appeared, both Betsy and Bo were in Paris, and their second round of battles with Plon Plon had begun. They had come fully prepared for their own private war. In fact, they had been gathering documents to support their claims for over three years. "My time," Betsy had written to John White in February 1861, "has been fully employed examining papers relative to our lawsuit." The process had clearly stirred many of her old resentments, for as she collected the letters and documents that told her story, the past imposed itself painfully on the present. Her letter to White focused as much on her father's unkind treatment and his humiliation of her in his will as it did on Plon Plon's machinations or the family council's injustices. And as she read Jérôme's letters once again, she saw "egotism and low meanness of character" where once she had seen only moral weakness.

Bo was meticulous in gathering his evidence for Berryer, providing letters dating back to 1803 between his mother, her husband, and others. He had translated the correspondence written in English into French for the lawyer. Along with these, he was prepared to provide all his own correspondence with the Bonaparte family, including a letter from Plon Plon, written before rivalry drove the two half brothers into enemy camps. "I am for life your devoted brother and friend," Plon Plon had declared—but it was no longer so.

Just as the battle over William Patterson's will had once reunited mother and son, now Betsy and Bo again found a cause that joined them. Together they busied themselves poring over the evidence they were readying for Berryer. As they worked, France seemed to buzz with excitement over the controversy produced by Jérôme's will. The distribution of Jérôme's worldly possessions was not dwelled upon in the press, for the king of Westphalia had lived his entire life far beyond his means. That life had ended, as it had begun, in dependence on support from relatives. His bequests did reveal, if only tangentially, his disregard for marital fidelity, for he provided a pension for his third and last wife, who had begun her relationship with him as his mistress while Catherine was alive. His daughter Princess Mathilde had received her share of her father's estate at the time of her marriage. A second son had died years before. As there was no mention in the will of Jérôme's first marriage or the family it had produced, Plon Plon emerged as his father's primary heir.

Although his father's estate might be small, Bo was determined to have his share of it. With Betsy, he filed a suit demanding an accounting, liquidation, and distribution of the deceased's estate. But money was not the issue that sparked the controversy in the minds of other Bonapartes. Jérôme's death led one of Lucien Bonaparte's sons to reopen the question: Who would succeed Louis-Napoleon? He requested a family council to sort out where members of his generation of Bonapartes stood in the line of succession. While this request was troublesome, it was not what concerned the family most. What sent Bonapartes scurrying to head off a confrontation was the possibility of a second challenge by Betsy and Bo.

Perhaps it was the emperor himself who tried to avert the crisis that everyone knew was brewing. Perhaps it was his wife. But Junior, who had remained in France when his father departed in 1857, was soon contacted by a gentleman who asked, in effect, what it would take to dissuade Bo from going to court over his legitimacy. The Bonapartes were willing to offer Betsy's son one-third of his father's estate if he would abandon his plans to press his claims of legitimacy.

There was an implicit threat in the letter Junior received. "I am confident," this intermediary wrote, "that the E. will do all in his power to prevent the suit, as it will produce much scandal." Junior declined to play any part in a scheme to silence his father. But he was astute enough to see that the emperor hoped to placate Plon Plon. It was a clear signal that Bo's half brother would have the upper hand in the events that would follow.

Despite the politics involved, Pierre Berryer believed he

could make a good legal case for the legality of Betsy's marriage and thus the legitimacy of her son. He was able to present to the court 139 pages of evidence, including proof of Betsy and Jérôme's marriage, the birth and baptism of their son, some sixty letters from members of the Bonaparte family recognizing Bo as a "dear son," "a nephew," or in Plon Plon's own case, "a cousin." The hearing began in January 1861, with both Betsy and Bo present in the courtroom.

Berryer's argument was, by all accounts, brilliant, moving, and convincing. He challenged Napoleon I's power to annul the marriage; he placed into evidence letters from Bonaparte family members, including Madame Mère, that demonstrated their acknowledgment of the legitimacy of the marriage; he cited Jérôme's letters to his young wife, assuring her of his faithfulness to her; he presented proof that the pope considered the marriage valid; and he reminded the court that the Civil Code forbade "the children of a second marriage to ask the nullity of the first during the lifetime of the parties to that marriage." He painted Betsy in the most sympathetic terms, telling the story of the romance and marriage between a young, naïve, and beautiful Baltimore girl and a handsome French naval officer, and of that husband's cruel abandonment of both wife and infant son. Although "Mademoiselle Patterson found herself repudiated—abandoned," she faced her betrayal with dignity, and for fifty-five years, she had led "a life without a stain." She never remarried but devoted herself, with "brave maternal love," to the child she had borne to her faithless husband. Now an elderly woman of seventy-five, "she comes from her distant home beyond the Atlantic; she appears before this august court asking for the declaration of her rights and demands the vindication of her honour and the establishment of her child in the position due to his birth."

Prince Napoleon's lawyer painted a far different story. The Patterson family knew from the beginning, he insisted, that Jérôme was a minor and could not marry without his family's permission. But they had entrapped this young, inexperienced boy, who had been so unfortunate as to visit Baltimore, a city known for vice and a "Sodom of impurities." Betsy must surely have been amazed to hear her native Baltimore, which she had always described as staid, boring, and utterly bourgeois, compared to the biblical city of immorality. She might have conceded, however, that her own father's "impurities" were many and that the memory of his infidelities still stung her. But Plon Plon's lawyer did not use William Patterson's mistresses as an example of Baltimore's sinfulness.

Instead, the lawyer moved to an attack on Betsy's character, a strategy designed to counter Berryer's image of an innocent and betrayed wife with a portrait of a conniving, selfish woman. He used the condemnation in William's will to paint her as a willful and disobedient daughter, inclined to foolish acts of misconduct. In the heat of oratory, perhaps the logical flaw in his argument slipped by the court: if the Patterson family had indeed conspired to entrap Jérôme Bonaparte in an invalid marriage, Betsy's role in the plot made her an obedient daughter rather than a rebellious child. This inconsistency in his argument passed without notice.

Betsy, he continued, was not simply willful or disobedient; she was greedy and a schemer. Proof could be found in her willingness to accept a pension from the first emperor Napoleon, a bald admission, he added, that her marriage to Jérôme was invalid. And he reminded the court that she had filed for and won a divorce in Maryland in 1812 for the sole reason, he insisted, that she wished to protect her growing personal wealth. The woman who emerged from his account was neither loyal nor devoted; she had burned with ambition in 1803—and she burned with it still. He begged the court to put an end to her dreams of power: uphold the family council's 1856 decision, he pleaded, and rule against the American Bonapartes.

As the trial progressed, Betsy had few friends with whom she could share her feelings of frustration, anger, and weariness. But chance brought her an opportunity to pour out her emotions to her old love, Alexander Gorchakov. Gorchakov had followed the trial in the papers and contacted Betsy. In a long letter, she vented her anger at her ex-husband. Perhaps, on reflection, she considered this too vicious and cold, for she later annotated it as "unsent." But perhaps her memory did not serve her well, for Gorchakov replied to her on the same day, February 19, that she penned a second letter in which her contempt for Jérôme was more muted. Still, she could not restrain herself from describing her former husband as a "personage, whose poverty of intellect . . . was exceeded by the littleness, baseness & meanness of his ignoble character." And as she noted sadly, his death had not ended her suffering at his hand, for Catherine's son continued to persecute her.

Gorchakov's reply offered sympathy and respect for Betsy's capacity for endurance and survival: "This drop in eternity that we call life has no greater value than the one that teaches us never to forsake our selves. This conviction was always embodied by you in every situation." His fondness for Betsy had endured, and he wrote feelingly of his regret that he no longer had "in my reach the fine and remarkable insights which I enjoyed there on the bank of the Arno, when public life did not yet have any thorns for me." His diplomatic duties weighed as heavily on him as her legal battles did on her; all he could do was recommend resignation to both their "desperately tried souls."

In the end, political considerations would once again desperately try Betsy's soul. The court's decision would rest not on Berryer's brilliant defense, or on the mountains of evidence presented by Betsy and her son, but on the complications that Bo's legitimacy would pose to the succession to the throne. Should anything befall Napoleon III's own son, the prince imperial, then Plon Plon was designated to wear the crown. Neither sympathy for an aging American woman nor the legality of her son's birth could outweigh the importance of ensuring a smooth transition of power. Thus, on February 15, 1861, the court handed down its decision against the American Bonapartes. But if anyone thought the Bonaparte family peace would not be disturbed again, they were wrong. Betsy and Bo remained confident that they had the better legal argument, and Berryer agreed. It was decided to appeal the case.

Throughout the spring and early summer, Betsy retained a

slim hope of achieving justice. But on July 1, 1861, the appeals court handed down its decision against the appellants. It found that the annulment of the marriage of Elizabeth Patterson and Jérôme Bonaparte was "in order and . . . unquestionably justified" and thus the case was "inadmissible." Betsy and Bo were ordered to pay a fine and to cover all the expenses incurred by the appeal. Thousands of dollars had been wasted, and their cause was lost.

Betsy's bitterness and disappointment were palpable. Once again political considerations had trumped legality. Almost six decades before, Napoleon had sacrificed her to his ambitions, and now the emperor and his nephew Plon Plon had sacrificed her to theirs. She could not respond with the resignation Prince Gorchakov had urged, for it did not suit her character. As she had once written to an English friend, she had never met fate "with Philosophy, resignation, or forgiveness, but . . . I did ever combat it with unbending courage." Yet she was realist enough to know that further efforts to establish Bo's legitimacy would be fruitless.

That summer Betsy sent her French lawyer a brief letter, in which her acceptance of defeat did not negate her fury. She advised him that she had urged her son "to follow my example of abstention from all further pursuit of that which is unattainable, justice from any court in France." The failure of her cause, she assured Berryer, could not be laid at his feet. "After the eminent talent, sir, which distinguishes yourself had failed before two courts to have our rights recognized, we ought to rest convinced that the Court of Cassation, equally servile, and curbed under the same pressure, would give the same illegal and unjust decision." And, writing to Bo, she declared, "I will never be dupe enough ever to try Justice in France under this Dynasty." She urged her son to take solace in their moral victory, for it was clear to her that "we have the Sympathies, from the Cottage to the palace of all France; & the opinion is universal that I, Mme P, have been most shamefully treated by the Bonaparte family from the First to this last advent of mine to France." With that, she packed her bags and returned to America. By August her ship had docked at New York—and she would not cross the ocean again.

Betsy's confidence that she and Bo had won in the court of public opinion, if not in the courts of France, was well founded. From the beginning, the series of trials and appeals had stirred strong responses, especially in the American and English press. Articles in the English papers found little to favor in the emperor or in Plon Plon or in the defense lawyer's arguments. Even before the final ruling on the case, an article in London's *Daily News* had criticized both Plon Plon and the man Betsy called "the Royal Bigamist." Articles like this one gave her confidence that the English press would "render me justice." And so it did: on the whole, the public expressed little sympathy for the late king of Westphalia or his second family.

Despite their victory in the trial, Prince Napoleon and Princess Mathilde were so embarrassed by the negative coverage in the press that they arranged for a highly favorable memoir of their father to be written and published shortly after the trial ended. But the *Memoirs and Correspondence of King Jérôme and*

Queen Catherine did little to stem the tide of criticism against Jérôme or his second family.

Betsy might have taken some satisfaction in reading the review of the memoir published that August in *The Athenaeum*. The review did not mince words when it came to Jérôme's character: he had, they wrote, "an unlimited faculty for spending money, [and] getting into debt and disgrace." He had begun life as a "spoiled, noisy, troublesome boy," and age did not improve him. Despite his title as king of Westphalia, Jérôme, it continued, hated responsibility and was never more than "a parvenu to the backbone, and his vulgarity was engrained. To appear in a state carriage, to receive attentions from high personages, to be flattered, to spend unlimited pocket-money, to have nothing to do but to go to *fetes* and public amusements, these were his notions of royal felicity."

But if the review dismissed Jérôme as a "fool and a poltroon" rather than a true villain, Betsy did not emerge as an innocent victim of love and betrayal. She was, the article conceded, "extremely beautiful . . . agreeable, witty, clever," but she was also ambitious. Indeed, "her character was not unlike Jerome's, in her love for all the vanities of life." She craved attention and admiration and "desired to shine in a wider horizon" than Baltimore, Maryland. True, she was young and might be forgiven her "female susceptibility" to a man to whom her own native country and the citizens of her native city were so eager to offer admiration and homage. But it was Betsy's desire to be envied by other women that banished any chance that good sense would prevail. And thus the marriage had taken place—and the betrayal had soon followed. In the end, the author of the review granted Betsy a measure of dignity; in the face of abandonment and humiliation, she had refused to be crushed. She had proved, as the years went by, "equal to her situation."

The commentary on her own desire for admiration and her delight at being envied would certainly have stung Betsy. And yet if she read this article, she could not have denied the truth of it. The vanity and ambition that had plunged a young girl into a disastrous marriage still lingered in an aging woman in the eighth decade of life.

Chapter Sixteen

"Once I Had Everything but Money; Now I Have Nothing but Money"

B etsy's war with the Bonapartes was over, but she had
returned to a nation at war with itself. She quickly discovered that her native state and city were as divided as the country, for Maryland's loyalties were fractured between Union and
Confederacy. Betsy's own family reflected this division: while
she, Bo, and her brother Edward cast their lot with the Union,
her only other surviving brother, George, remained a proud
slave owner.

Betsy opposed "this vile Rebellion," but it did not spark in
her the same passions that events in France had always roused.
When she spoke of it at all, it was to remark upon its foolishness. Writing to a friend in France, she could only lament
the poor judgment that had brought the country to devasta-
tion and bloodshed. "I can tell you nothing of the Politics of
this unhappy Country," she confessed. "I can only sigh over
the fatality which impelled my blind fellow Citizens to anni-
hilate the prosperity of their once promising greatness . . . by
cutting the throats of Each other." It was true that all around
her she saw evidence of the destruction of that prosperity: business in Baltimore was at a standstill, tenants could not pay their
rent, and buildings had fallen into disrepair. By August 1861, the

entire state of Maryland was under martial law, and neighbors who were open sympathizers with the Confederacy were fearful of imprisonment.

Betsy was determined that her own throat would not be one of those slashed by the Civil War. If her real estate was losing value, if many of the houses she owned in Baltimore were falling apart, she would find a new source of income to compensate for her losses. She had always been a shrewd if cautious investor, and now, setting aside her anger at the French courts, she turned her attention to her finances. She decided to purchase federal government securities. The war might be foolish, but the profits to be made from these government bonds might well make her fortune.

Betsy's investment strategy paid off; by war's end, she was close to being a millionaire. Where once, in 1849, she had received only $10,000 a year, now her investments spun off $100,000 each year. The irony of this circumstance was not lost on her: "Once I had everything but money," she was reported to have said; "now I have nothing but money."

The comment was smart and clever but far from accurate. The now-lost "everything" that she spoke of undoubtedly referred to her youth, her beauty, and her ambitions, both for herself and for her son, Bo. But she surely had not forgotten the periods of loneliness, ennui, anxiety, and anger at her father and her former husband; the memories haunted her as much as the need to manage her meager finances. No amount of money could have altered the humiliation of her father's will, the heartbreak of a hopeless romance with Prince Gorchakov, or the betrayal she felt when Bo married Susan Williams.

Her present condition was far from perfect—she had grown old, her hopes of vindication had been cruelly dashed, and she had accepted the fact that she would live out the remainder of her life where it had begun, in Baltimore. But wealth was not all she could point to in her current life. Age had certainly been kind to her; in 1870, when Betsy was eighty-five, the local newspaper reported that she "retains TRACES OF A ONCE WONDROUS BEAUTY. Her complexion is still smooth and comparatively fair, while her peculiarly beautiful blue eyes are as yet undimmed." Men, like John Perkergrue, still wrote love poems to her. Others, including the persistent John R. Prichard, proposed marriage. Prichard's affections were thoroughly unwelcome; on his many letters, Betsy wrote comments such as "an unknown Madman and idiot." Perhaps, of course, these suitors were drawn to her for her wealth as much as for her beautiful blue eyes. No matter; she had at last found a perfect companion—and someone to dote on: her second grandchild, Charles Bonaparte.

Charley, now in his twenties, was a study in contrast with his older brother, Junior. As a young man, Junior had been dashing, handsome, and virile, a soldier and a war hero; Charles was rather stocky, serious, and studious, cut out for the law office rather than the battlefield. But Betsy discovered that she and this grandson shared in common a caustic wit, and this surely pleased and amused her. As he grew up and she grew older, she came to rely upon him to manage her finances and her legal affairs. Later he would enter President Theodore Roosevelt's cabinet as attorney general and establish the precursor to the Federal Bureau of Investigation.

But blows came in the 1870s that deepened Betsy's bitterness and robbed her of any focus on the future. In 1870 she became a parent who outlived her own child, for in that year her only son, Bo, died. The following year Junior dealt her a crushing blow when he, like his father before him, chose to marry an American woman. The shock Betsy felt was great. For despite her defeat in the French courts, despite Plon Plon's influence over Napoleon III, and despite all evidence that her ambition had been permanently thwarted, Betsy could not entirely abandon the dreams that had for so long defined her life. Against all logic, she still harbored a hope that a member of her family might someday, somehow, enter the ranks of European aristocracy or sit in a seat of European power. For over a decade, that hope had been pinned on Junior. Over the years, she had showered upon this grandson the money needed to maintain a suitable aristocratic lifestyle. She had paid for horses, carriages, elegant dwellings, and well-tailored uniforms. But in 1871, after Prussia defeated France in the 1870 war and as the Second French Empire crumbled around him, the younger Jerome Napoleon Bonaparte returned to the United States and took an American wife.

Betsy's anger and despair at the news blinded her to any consideration of Junior's happiness. She saw his decision, as she had seen his father's, as an affront, a blow to her, struck thoughtlessly and without justification. "The humiliating Shame & Mortification heaped on myself by Relations," she wrote to the bridegroom, "amount to Fatality, from which there is no escape." His future, she assured him, would forever be bleak: "I pity you because the remainder of your disgraced position will be a lingering remorseful agony." And among the consequences of the marriage, perhaps the most dire was "an eternal separation from the Best friend, Myself, whom you ever possessed. I will never admit Mrs. Edgar or yourself to my presence." To this threat of banishment, she added another: she would cut off the generous allowance she had sent him in the past. In her anger, she spoke in a voice that ought to have been familiar to her— the voice of her father.

Junior's wife, a widow with three children, came from a distinguished American family, for she was the granddaughter of Daniel Webster. This mattered little to Betsy. She could not forget that she and her grandchildren were Bonapartes. She was "filled with astonishment & regret" that her grandson had so quickly forgotten his heritage. He had made a marriage, she wrote him, "entirely beneath your position in the world & your name." Decades before, when Betsy had left Baltimore for Britain, William had declared that action proof that she was mentally unbalanced. Now his disobedient daughter passed the same judgment on her grandson. Only madness, she concluded, could explain this tragic turn of events.

Betsy's anger burned brightly, but it soon abated. Her threats were largely forgotten, and she made her peace with her grandson just as she had made her peace with her son. Yet the loss of her dreams, foolish though they had been for many years, cast a pall over her remaining years. She grew more eccentric, more bitter, and she seemed to live more in the past than in the present, except where her money was concerned. She engaged in battles with ghosts, writing a *Dialogue of the Dead; or, Dialogues Between Jerome and My Father in Hell,* in which the souls of her father and her husband sparred with each other, and she continued her quarrels with her father, Nancy Spear, and others by annotating the letters she had received from them or sent to them over her lifetime.

The newspaper reporter who had praised Betsy's continuing beauty in 1870 had also commented astutely on the wariness and defensiveness that enveloped her in old age. "Her nature is suspicious and warped by many injuries," he observed. "She seems in constant dread of some indefinable injury. . . . [She] is always on the watch for some fancied insult." This wariness and dread had, it was true, been earned over her lifetime, yet as she entered her eighties and nineties, it seemed to define her too fully.

Betsy knew that she had outlived both friends and enemies. William was dead. Her husband and her son and all her brothers were dead. Her closest confidante, Sydney Morgan, had died in 1859, in the midst of Betsy's legal battles in France. History had passed her by. The young and brash republic she had grown up in was taking its place on the world stage as an industrial giant. The domesticity that she had feared would smother her was giving way to a surprising array of public roles for women and to an organized demand for full citizenship for her sex. The name Bonaparte, which had once prompted fear and admiration, was rarely heard in the halls of power. And for a young generation of Europeans as well as Americans, wealth rather than bloodline or breeding had become the measure of a man.

Betsy had also outlived her own celebrity. Her marriage and her divorce had once been the subject of political debate inside and outside Congress. Her story had been told over and over again, in the early decades of the century and again in the 1850s and 1860s, when the succession to the French throne had been in question. When Jérôme died, newspapers had filled their columns with accounts of the fairy-tale marriage that had ended so tragically, and when Bo died, the story had been told once again. But many of the people who saw Betsy in the streets of Baltimore in her final years, walking with her red parasol and her embroidered bag on her arm, as she collected her rents and visited her brokers' offices, viewed her as a curiosity, a relic of a past they did not have time to give much thought to.

As she entered her nineties, Betsy's health at last began to fail. Her digestive tract could tolerate little but brandy and milk. On Christmas Day 1878, she made her last trip down the stairs of her boardinghouse. Five days later she was bedridden. As the doctor readied his diagnosis, her wit once again flared; she knew what was wrong with her, she told him: my illness is old age. Both Junior and Charles came to her bedside and were with her when, at midday on April 4, 1879, Elizabeth Patterson Bonaparte died. Her death prompted a last, fleeting moment of celebrity, as newspapers across the country carried brief notices of her passing. Perhaps the local Baltimore paper captured the moment best: "She passed away quietly this afternoon. Close of a long and Strangely Interesting Career."

Betsy had taken steps to ensure that she would have the last word in her long battle with her father and her brothers.

She left instructions not to bury her in the family cemetery at Coldstream; instead, she had chosen a plot in the Greenmount Cemetery. "I have been alone in life," she wrote as her own epitaph, "and I wish to be alone in death." But well-meaning relatives robbed her of even this small victory over William and Jérôme and all those who had criticized or betrayed her, for on her tombstone they carved only a platitude: "After life's fitful fever she sleeps well."

"I Have Lived Alone and I Will Die Alone"

Elizabeth Patterson Bonaparte was an American celebrity, perhaps the first of her era. That celebrity rested on her connection to the family of one of the nineteenth century's most powerful and charismatic figures, Napoleon Bonaparte. The press, both in America and Europe, told and retold the story of her marriage to Jérôme Bonaparte each time a link could be found between this American beauty and the family that dominated Europe for decades. The whirlwind romance was news when her husband abandoned her, and again when he died, when she sued in the French courts for the acknowledgment of her son's legitimacy, and yet again when she died at the age of ninety-four. As the narrative became one of innocence betrayed and rejected, Betsy's life became emblematic of the dangers of the New World's continuing romance with the Old.

It is not surprising that Betsy's story captured the attention of Americans. For in the beginning, it was indeed the stuff that fairy tales are made of. Its heroine was remarkably beautiful, and she won the attention of a suitor who seemed, on the surface, to be a prince charming. Jérôme was dashing, worldly— and the opposition to the marriage mounted by her father and by French officials in America added to the romance of their courtship. Betsy was too young and too headstrong to see that

Jérôme was egotistical, irresponsible, and a womanizer. Had the marriage not been annulled by Napoleon, it might have dissolved under the weight of her realization that sometimes a prince is only a frog in a velvet coat. But it was not Jérôme's character flaws that captured the public's attention; it was the sacrifice of the marriage at the altar of Napoleon's ambition that ensured the lasting celebrity of Jérôme's "American wife." It was the tragedy of being Elizabeth Patterson Bonaparte that her nation chose to remember until her death.

This narrow focus on the relationship between Elizabeth Patterson and Jérôme Bonaparte is a different sort of tragedy. For lost in the tale of a woman seduced and abandoned is the story of a woman who created a remarkable life for herself. In an era that was beginning to laud the self-made man, Elizabeth Patterson Bonaparte stood as that rarity, a self-made woman. Denied a fortune by her father and by Napoleon, she made one for herself, amassing well over a million and a half dollars through a lifetime of careful budgeting and clever investment in real estate and government bonds. Denied entrée into Europe's most elite society on the arm of a husband, she won admission to this closed circle of privilege and bloodline by dazzling the aristocrats, artists, and intellectuals of the continent with her wit and intelligence as well as her beauty. As much as Napoleon, she might have boasted that she was the fabricator of her own destiny.

Lost too is the complexity of Elizabeth Patterson Bonaparte's personality and character. In her letters to family and friends, she laid waste to American culture and to America's gender ideals. She decried the narrowness and emptiness of a society whose men focused on moneymaking to the exclusion of all else and whose women were emotionally confined to the parlor and the nursery, to accommodating their husbands and raising their children. She embraced European aristocratic society, with its leadership built upon bloodlines, its appreciation for artistic and intellectual achievement, and its validation of a public, social role for women. Again and again she declared the superiority of this European culture over the narrow, humdrum, confining, and unsophisticated society of her native land. And yet Betsy's own behavior often belied her rejection of all things American. In the same letters that carried her contempt for the American man, imprisoned in his countinghouse and obsessed with gains and losses, she often revealed her own meticulous and focused attention to money and moneymaking. She issued careful and detailed instructions to financial agents to buy or sell real estate, stocks, and bonds; she considered exchange rates and interest rates in her transactions; and she adjusted her investment strategy in the light of political and economic developments on both continents. Her fortune grew and, with it, an obsession with wealth and its acquisition that would have won the admiration of any American man.

Betsy never saw the contradiction in her simultaneous condemnation and embrace of the American entrepreneurial and mercantile spirit. Nor did she see the contradiction in her contempt for the maternal sacrifices required of domesticity and her own devotion to and sacrifice for her son and grandsons. She also remained unaware of the contradictions in the values she hoped to impart to her son. She preached the importance of his bloodline in determining his destiny and took pains to provide him with aristocratic manners and attitudes, yet at the same time she prepared him for life in the American meritocracy, confident that a good education and the professional opportunities it could provide were the path to his economic independence. Bo reconciled these mixed signals by marrying wealth rather than earning it, by taking an aristocratic attitude toward work and its rewards in a decidedly American setting.

Perhaps the most tragic unacknowledged contradiction lay in Betsy's relationship with her father. Their contest of wills, their overt condemnation of each other's life choices and personal behavior, ironically attested to their intense emotional connection. Betsy consistently tried to win her father's approval; William consistently tried to win her respect. Neither succeeded, and the final bond between them was forged from anger, bitterness, and contempt.

Although Betsy enjoyed no formal political rights and wielded no formal political power, she was nevertheless influential in the political and diplomatic decision making of the early republic. Her connection to the most powerful man in Europe, the emperor of France, made her personal life not simply grist for the popular press but a matter of concern in the halls of Congress and a factor in the diplomacy of American presidents and ambassadors. In the imperial struggles of the 1790s and the early decades of the nineteenth century, both France and England employed the carrot and the stick to move the United States away from its policy of neutrality. The American public and its government were ambivalent, shifting support from one side to the other in the face of real and perceived insults to the nation's sovereignty. British ambassadors and French consuls eagerly looked for signs of support or opposition, not simply in proclaimed policies but in such small matters as the seating at a dinner party or an invitation to a ball. In such a fraught environment, many of the most personal events in Betsy's life— her marriage to a Bonaparte, Napoleon's rejection of its legitimacy, the rumors of her remarriage to an Englishman, and the pension granted to her by Napoleon—each became a potential diplomatic crisis. Decades after Napoleon's death, her actions caused concern and anxiety within the halls of power in France. By demanding that her son be recognized as legitimate, she threatened to disrupt the Bonaparte family's agreed-upon line of succession during the reign of Napoleon III. Betsy's story thus reminds us that policies are often formed at the nexus of the private and the public spheres.

By the time of her death, many of the once-unique aspects of Betsy's life had become commonplace. In the late nineteenth and early twentieth centuries, American writers from Henry James to Edith Wharton built novels around characters who were easily recognizable within post–Civil War society: eligible young women like Conchita Closson, Nan St. George, and Lizzy Elmsworth in Wharton's *The Buccaneers,* who sought to acquire a European husband and, with him, a title; or the tragic Isabel Archer of James's *Portrait of a Lady,* who, like Betsy, was willing to "confront her destiny" in a European setting. Even before the war, Americans of both sexes found their way in

droves to the delights and wonders of Europe's cities and countryside, making the "Grand Tour" de rigueur for all well-bred
citizens. Beginning in the 1830s, the nation came to tolerate,
if not entirely accept, middle-class women who chose not to
marry but to devote themselves to causes and sometimes even to
careers. These women, like Betsy, managed the money on which
they lived and by which they brought about social change. And
in the factories and mills and servants' quarters, single women
who depended on their own incomes understood—as Betsy
had—the connection between money and a measure of independence. If Betsy had once shocked matrons and gentlemen
alike by appearing in public in the new French Empire–style
gown that allowed only the wispiest of undergarments, by the
1850s the bloomer costume defied notions of female modesty
even further by placing women in pants. And by the 1840s,
articulate groups of women challenged the tenets of domesticity that confined married women to their duties in the home.
From the Seneca Falls Convention in 1848, to the founding of
national suffrage associations in the wake of the Fourteenth
Amendment, to the concerted push for suffrage that began in
Betsy's last years, she could see emerging around her, had she
wished to look, a critique of domesticity that was social and
legal rather than simply personal.

The fact that American society, and American women in
particular, were catching up with Betsy does not diminish the
power of her story. All alone she challenged the life her father
and her society had expected her to follow. She rebounded from
the disillusionment and humiliation that followed her one act

of folly—marriage to Jérôme Bonaparte—and she refused to put her future into the hands of a man ever again. In an age when proper women did not venture far from home without an escort or a husband, she crossed the Atlantic several times and traveled through Europe by herself. And in those early decades of the nineteenth century, when women's names rarely appeared in newspapers, she gloried in her celebrity. She never suppressed her wit or her intelligence and was as proud of her independence and ability to provide for herself as any self-made man. And she remained tenacious in her demands for justice from the Bonapartes, challenging them in public, in a court of law, to acknowledge the legitimacy of her marriage and of her son.

Betsy paid dearly for her choices in life, of course. The disillusionment she suffered as a young woman began as a source of wisdom and sophistication, but in her later years, it became deeply tinged by jealousy at the good fortune of others. Her habit of economy, the product of a desire to be independent, showed overtones as she aged of mere miserliness. Bitterness never marked her face, but it had begun in the 1850s to mar her spirit, and she wrote her own history not as a triumph over adversity but as a chain of endless disappointments and betrayals. Perhaps saddest of all, her obsession with her son's and grandsons' destinies blinded her to considerations of their happiness or their satisfactions. Her life was defined by the fact that she was an American Bonaparte, and this proved to be a burden that neither she nor her son and grandsons could escape. She took little pride in the respect that the Baltimore community showed to her son or in the financial success of her grandson Junior. Junior's marriage to the granddaughter of one of the nation's most prominent political figures, Daniel Webster, failed to satisfy Betsy's ambition for her family. By her rigid social yardstick, neither Daniel Webster's fame as an orator nor his influence as a Massachusetts senator during the decades before the Civil War could measure up to the achievements of the European noblemen she had known. Her insistence on the special destiny of her family would have also deprived her of satisfaction in the career of her seaside companion, Charley. Charley would lift the Bonaparte name to national political prominence in the twentieth century, but for Betsy, the only political landscape suitable for a Bonaparte lay across the ocean in Europe. It would have pleased her more to learn that Junior's daughter, Louise Eugenie, gained a title when she married a Danish count.

Shortly before her death, Elizabeth Patterson Bonaparte, the most beautiful woman in America, summed up her life: "I have lived alone and I will die alone." Surely the combination of pride and bitterness captured by this comment cannot be lost upon those of us who know her story.

The American Bonapartes

For almost a quarter century after Betsy Bonaparte's death, her family faded from the public eye. By 1879 the Bonaparte sun had been eclipsed in Europe as well, and a president rather than an emperor was in place in France. In America, public attention turned to the rise of millionaire industrialists, labor unrest, the flood of immigrants from southern Europe, and the return of white southerners to power after the abandonment of Reconstruction—and American newspapers were filled with muckraking articles decrying political bosses, unsanitary food processing, and the plight of the men and women in the slums. The battlefield heroics of Betsy's grandson Junior, which had won him medals and honors during the Crimean War, were little remembered by a society busily commissioning statues and plaques to commemorate their Civil War dead.

The American Bonapartes seemed to settle into their anonymity with sighs of relief. Junior, who resigned his commission in the French cavalry and returned to his native country, appeared content to enjoy the prosperous and respectable life relished by his father and his maternal grandfather before him. With his wife, Caroline Leroy Appleton Edgar Bonaparte, the granddaughter of one of antebellum America's greatest orators and political figures, Daniel Webster, Junior lived out the century as a businessman, released at last from his grandmother's ambitions.

By the time Junior's son, the fourth to carry the name Jerome Bonaparte, came of age, the burden of Betsy's ambitions had been entirely lifted. This Jerome entertained no thoughts of an active connection to his European relatives; he was American born and bred. In 1914, as a new war appeared on Europe's horizon, he married an American divorcée and made his home in Washington, D.C. The only member of the Bonaparte family to achieve a place in European nobility was his sister, Louise Eugenie, who married a Danish count, Adam Comte de Molke-Huitfeldt. When she died in 1923, at the age of forty-nine, she left behind five children who were not newsworthy in America.

William Patterson's devotion to respectability seemed to run in the veins of Betsy's descendants, but there were signs that her pride in bearing the name Bonaparte was not entirely absent. Her son, after all, could be seen until his death in 1870 riding in an elegant carriage that carried his mother's unofficial coat of arms on its doors. And his grandson raised his family in a home on Washington's K Street so lavish that neighbors dubbed it "Chateau Bonaparte."

Still, it was not a Jerome but a Charles Bonaparte who brought the family name to national prominence once again. This second son of Jerome and Susan Bonaparte, born twenty years after his older brother, grew up in a new, modernizing America, far more confident of itself than the fledgling republic that had seen potential danger in a seventeen-year-old's marriage to Napoleon's brother. Charles was a Harvard junior in

1871, the year his brother married and Napoleon III lost his throne. As a young boy, Charley had been Betsy Bonaparte's favorite oceanside companion, and as an adult, he became her trusted business manager. But in 1875 he too disappointed his grandmother by taking Ellen Channing Day, the daughter of an attorney, as his wife.

Charles was a lawyer—and by all accounts a brilliant one. He opened his practice in Baltimore, but having inherited a fortune from his grandmother, he had no need to take on cases that brought in huge fees. Instead he established himself as a champion of justice. He joined the Baltimore Reform League and the Maryland Civil Service League, thus aligning himself with one of the major reform efforts of the Gilded Age. With other civil service reformers, he campaigned to replace a patronage system that led to the corrupt and inefficient operations of government with a nonpartisan test of competency for appointees. The Pendleton Act of 1883 marked the movement's first major success. In 1889 Charles met Theodore Roosevelt, who was then serving on the relatively new Civil Service Commission. The two Harvard alums became close friends, and when Roosevelt became president, he appointed Charles Bonaparte to the Board of Indian Commissioners. Soon afterward he made Charles a special prosecutor in cases of fraud in the postal service. By 1905 Charles Bonaparte had entered Roosevelt's cabinet as secretary of the navy, and the following year, at age forty-five, he was sworn in as U.S. attorney general.

As attorney general, Charles produced an impressive record. He appeared before the Supreme Court more than five hundred times and delivered more than a hundred opinions on a broad range of legal matters to the president. His prosecution of cases under the antitrust laws earned him a national reputation as one of Teddy Roosevelt's "trust busters." During his years with the Justice Department, he mounted a crusade to improve law enforcement by creating special agents under his direction. The result was a Bureau of Investigation; its agents became known as "G Men," and the bureau was the precursor of the FBI.

Charles retired from national public office when Roosevelt's second term ended. He returned to Baltimore and to his law practice, but he remained an active supporter of the reform of government. He founded the National Municipal League and served as its president. His reputation continued to grow, as a judge of the U.S. Court of Appeals later put it, because he was "an honest-to-goodness, dyed-in-the-wool, brash reformer." An outpouring of books, essays, and articles on reform by Charles seemed to confirm this view. Yet Charles's devotion to clean government did not arise from a humanitarian or philanthropic philosophy. He was, in the spirit of William Patterson, an advocate of individual responsibility and a strong opponent of public assistance to the poor. He earned the nickname "Soup House Charlie" in the 1880s when he declared that a public school system was undesirable and "as ridiculous . . . as . . . free soup kitchens." As one reporter astutely observed, Charles Bonaparte was a walking contradiction: "by instinct a royalist, by profession a democrat and a reformer."

Physically, Charley did not resemble either the Bonaparte or the Patterson line. True, he was said to have a "Bonaparte smile" and the small hands and feet of his grandmother, but he was a large and sturdy man, with a bull neck and a massive head. His combination of physical and intellectual superiority was captured in the description of that "vast round, rugged head, a double-decker head; a cannon ball head, like a warrior's, with room for two sets of brains." His personality, however, reflected a remarkable blending of William Patterson's moral certitude and judgmental impulses and his grandmother's charm and sarcasm. He was comfortable sitting in judgment of others, and many of his books and essays focused on the need to rid the nation of men he labeled public or private sinners. He was admired for his witty repartee, heavily laced as it was with sarcasm, and as one observer noted, he was a man of great wit but no sense of humor. He was a favorite of newspaper reporters, who liked to interview him, not simply because of his high profile in Teddy Roosevelt's government or his prominence in reform organizations, but because he was "good copy." He spoke his mind; he did not mince words; and he did not care if his opinions brought criticism down upon him.

With Charles, any lingering connection to the European Bonapartes was finally severed. He responded coolly when told he resembled the famous Napoleon, and he distanced himself from the history of the family in France by declaring he came from Italian and Scottish stock and did not have a drop of French blood in his veins. He never visited France or made any effort to contact European relatives. His concerns, while he served in the national government and after his retirement from office, were entirely American: conservation, Indian affairs, regulation of trusts, efficient criminal investigation, and civil service reform. The rise and fall of kings and European governments were matters of only mild and passing interest.

Charles Bonaparte died in 1921. He had no children, and thus his line in the family genealogy ended with his death. In his spirited devotion to a single cause, Charles most closely resembled his grandmother, and like her, he achieved national prominence for this American branch of the Bonaparte family.

Acknowledgments

Most writers like to think of their work as a solitary endeavor, but this is an illusion. When we sit down to write that section of a book called "Acknowledgments," we realize that every book is a collaborative effort. And for me, this has never been more true than in the writing of Elizabeth Patterson Bonaparte's biography.

The idea of telling Betsy's story came from my good friend, the talented scriptwriter of many PBS documentaries, Ronald Blumer. Ron encountered Betsy while working on a show about her good friend Dolley Madison. He e-mailed me and suggested—no, ordered—that I tell Betsy's story. I heard, and I obeyed.

Betsy's papers, as well as many of the Patterson family papers, are in the Maryland Historical Society archives. The society's Lord Baltimore Fellowship allowed me the time and resources to plumb their rich collections. The Johns Hopkins University's History Department's grant of a visiting professorship opened the university's libraries to me as well. My work there was made easier by the willingness of my niece, Laurie Berkin, to sign on as my unpaid research assistant. In addition to helping me go through the many boxes of Betsy's letters, Laurie proved expert at locating the best crabcakes in Baltimore. Soon after I returned from Maryland, Eric Herschthal, now a graduate student at Columbia University, volunteered to do research for me. He scoured secondary sources on everything from Haitian refugees in Baltimore, to the architecture of the city in the eighteenth century, to minor Jeffersonian-era political figures. When I was stymied over how to locate an obscure journal article, I could always turn to Michael Hattem, a brilliant former Baruch student, now getting his Ph.D. in history at Yale. Michael's investigative skills are remarkable, as are his computer skills. I have him on speed dial for all the technological problems that terrify members of my generation. Raoul Boisset, a Baruch College senior with a French background, translated some of the trickier paragraphs in letters to Betsy, as did Kimberly Adams, my friend in Guilford, Connecticut, whose knowledge of nineteenth-century French slang is most impressive. When it was all done, another excellent graduate student, Laura Ping, helped me get my endnotes in their proper form.

Friends and colleagues played a major role in seeing this book to completion. From the first outline to the last written page, Professors Cindy Lobel, Angelo Angelis, and Philip Papas read the manuscript and offered their usual tough criticism, scribbled on the draft pages I sent them and shared over cake and coffee or a glass of wine. They have been the guiding spirits of my last three books—and I have given them tenure in that role. Margaret Berlin, Landa Freeman, and Julie Des Jardins read chapters as they came off the computer—and read them again, sometimes in their third and even fourth iterations. They took their duties seriously, correcting grammar and punctuation and writing "unclear" or "why?" in the margins on many a page. Margaret was gloriously relentless, and even on our daily summer walks in Connecticut, she pursued her points without breaking stride. Much that is good in this book—and none of what the reader might find wanting—can be attributed to the assistance of these friends, students, and colleagues.

Dozens of teachers—from Colorado to Washington, D.C., to Fort Lauderdale, Bridgeport, and Huntsville—listened to me talk about Betsy at the faculty development programs made possible by Teaching American History grants. Their questions and comments were invaluable, for my goal in recent years has been to reach a broader audience than my colleagues in academe. It is a shame that this grants program has vanished, for it provided a rare opportunity for scholars and teachers to share their love of history.

Ana Calero, who keeps the history department running smoothly at Baruch, and who has endured my shrieks of "I can't make the printer work" for many years, patiently assisted me once again in printing out copies of the manuscript.

Dan Green, my agent and friend, read every word, as he always does, and made astute comments—as he always does. His gentle nudges—"How's the book coming?"—were invaluable in stirring the guilt that helps authors finish a project. My thanks too to my editor at Knopf, Victoria Wilson, and to her assistant Daniel Schwartz, as well as to the copy editor, Janet Biehl, who refined my wilder sentence constructions and judiciously added or eliminated commas and colons.

Finally, my thanks to my family, which has expanded to

include not only my daughter, Hannah, and son, Matthew, but their spouses, Eamon and Jessica, to whom this book is dedicated. These four remarkable young adults have brought me great joy, a reasonable amount of gray hair, and a new knowledge of the subway routes to their neighborhoods in Brooklyn. It saddens me to think that Elizabeth Patterson Bonaparte never experienced the delight that only a loving family can provide.

—Carol Berkin

Notes

1 "She Is a Most Extraordinary Girl"

4 By July 1778: See Helen Jean Burn, *Betsy Bonaparte* (Baltimore: Maryland Historical Society, 2010), pp. 6–23, for a full discussion of William Patterson's early years and his marriage to Dorcas Spear.

5 In choosing Dorcas: Virginia Tatnall Peacock, *Famous American Belles of the Nineteenth Century* (Books for Libraries Press, n.d., reissued by University, 2011), p. 41.

5 "What I possess": Ibid., p. 42

6 As a husband: E. M. Oddie, *The Bonapartes in the New World* (London: Elkin Mathews and Marrot, 1932), p. 6, describes William as "a dour, self righteous, God-fearing man, who liked laying down the law sententiously to his fellows, and keeping his household in order."

6 "We treat women": F. M. Kicheisen, *Memoirs of Napoleon the First Compiled from His Writing* (New York: Duffield & Co., 1929), p. 152.

7 Dorcas's first daughter: Inventory made by Elizabeth Patterson Bonaparte [hereafter EPB], August 11, 1838, Maryland Historical Society [MdHS], ms. 142.

8 Betsy dreamed of: Annie Leakin Sioussat, *Old Baltimore* (New York: Macmillan, 1931), pp. 133–34.

8 When she was ten: Oddie, *Bonapartes in the New World,* pp. 7–8; Claude Bourguignon-Frasseto, *Betsy Bonaparte: The Belle of Baltimore* (Baltimore: Maryland Historical Society, 2003), pp. 7–9.

9 "I always considered": William Patterson's Will, MdHS, ms. 645

10 "She is a most extraordinary": Rosalie Stier Calvert to her mother, 1803, in Margaret Law Callcott, ed., *Mistress of Riversdale: The Plantation Letters of Rosalie Stier Calvert* (Baltimore: Johns Hopkins University Press, 1991), p. 62.

10 "No sovereign":, William W. Stowe, *Going Abroad: European Travel in Nineteenth-Century American Culture* (Princeton, N.J.: Princeton University Press, 1994), p. 5.

11 "I most solemnly": Nicholas Smith to EPB, February 1802, MdHS, ms. 142.

12 As a child: For a sympathetic but not uncritical biography of Jérôme Bonaparte, see Philip Walsingham Sergeant, *Jérôme Bonaparte: The Burlesque Napoleon; Being the Story of the Life and Kingship of the Youngest Brother of Napoleon the Great* (Whitefish, Mont.: Kessinger, 2005). Sergeant, who describes Jérôme as a "monumental rake," notes that "his chief claim to notoriety lies in the fact that . . . he distinguished himself by the pernacity of his gallantry." See also Clarence Edward McCartney and Gordon Dorrance, *The Bonapartes in America* (Philadelphia: Dorrance & Co., 1939), pp. 32–33.

13 "I am like that": Sergeant, *Jérôme Bonaparte*, p. 14; Laure Junot Abrantès, *At the Court of Napoleon: Memoirs of the Duchesse d'Abrantès* (Gloucester, U.K.: Windrush Press, 1989), pp. 46–54.

13 Jérôme's character: Sidney Mitchell, *A Family Lawsuit: The Romantic Story of Elisabeth Patterson and Jérôme Bonaparte* (New York: Farrar, Straus and Cudahy, 1958), p. 24.

13 "You brought him up": Abrantès, *At the Court of Napoleon,* pp. 132–33.

13 "Signora Letizia spoils": Ibid.

14 Jérôme's arrival in America: Sergeant, *Jérôme Bonaparte,* chaps. 2 and 3.

15 One of the few: Mitchell, *Family Lawsuit,* pp. 32–34.

16 But there are other: For the various accounts, see Oddie, *Bonapartes in the New World,* pp. 13–14; Burn, *Betsy Bonaparte,* pp. 42–43; Dorothy MacKay Quynn, "The Marriage of Betsy Patterson and Jérôme Bonaparte," unpublished ms., MdHS, chap. 1.

17 Though young, Jérôme Bonaparte: According to one contemporary, Jérôme received three challenges to duel because of his flaunting of American courtship rules. See Richard Beale Davis, ed., *Jeffersonian America: Notes on the United States of America Collected in the Years 1805–6–7 and 11–12 by Sir Augustus John Foster, Bart.* (San Marino, Calif.: Huntington Library, 1954), p. 65.

2 *"I Would Rather Be the Wife of Jérôme Bonaparte for an Hour"*

18 "I would rather": E. M. Oddie, *The Bonapartes in the New World* (London: Elkin Mathews and Marrot, 1932), p. 22; Dorothy MacKay Quynn, "The Marriage of Betsy Patterson and Jérôme Bonaparte," unpublished ms., MdHS, chap. 2; Geraldine Brooks, *Dames and Daughters of the Young Republic* (General Books, 2009), p. 58.

19 Although William grudgingly: For an account of Jérôme's flirtations, see Richard Beale Davis, ed., *Jeffersonian America: Notes on the United States of America Collected in the Years 1805–6–7 and 11–12 by Sir Augustus John Foster, Bart.* (San Marino, Calif.: Huntington Library, 1954), p. 65.

20 Family members now: John Pancake, *Samuel Smith and the Politics of Business, 1782–1839* (Tuscaloosa: University of Alabama Press, 1972), pp. 70; Thomas Armstrong, *Politics, Diplomacy and Intrigue in the Early Republic: The Cabinet Career of Robert Smith, 1801–1811* (Dubuque, Ia.: Kendall Hunt, 1991), pp. 9–10.

20 Beleaguered from many sides: Articles of Agreement and Settlement, December 24, 1803, MdHS, ms. 142.

21 "not without importance": James Madison to Robert R. Livingston, MdHS, ms. 142. See William Thomas Roberts Saffell, *The Bonaparte-Patterson Marriage in 1803* (General Books, 2009), chap. 2, for a full discussion of the diplomatic implications.

23 "a man of the fairest character": Thomas Jefferson to Robert R. Livingston, November 4, 1803, in Paul Leicester Ford, ed., *The Works of Thomas Jefferson in Twelve Volumes.* Vol. 10, *Correspondence and Papers, 1803–1807* (New York: G. P. Putnam's Sons, 1904–5), p. 50.

23 Still, not all of William's: Oddie, *Bonapartes in the New World*, p. 19; the legality of the marriage is discussed at length in Saffell, *Bonaparte-Patterson Marriage.*

24 "Is it possible, sir": Ibid., pp. 29–30.

25 "driven off to one": Rosalie Stier Calvert to Mme. H. J. Stier, n.d., November 1803, in Margaret Law Callcott, ed., *Mistress of Riversdale: The Plantation Letters of Rosalie Stier Calvert* (Baltimore: Johns Hopkins University Press, 1991), pp. 61–63.

26 It was now clear: Sidney Mitchell, *A Family Lawsuit: The Romantic Story of Elisabeth Patterson and Jérôme Bonaparte* (New York: Farrar, Straus and Cudahy, 1958), p. 43.

26 "if the marriage": Eugène Lemoine Didier, *The Life and Letters of Madame Bonaparte* (Chestnut Hill, Mass.: Adamant Media, 2005, replica of 1879 edition), p. 16.

26 At the ceremony: Oddie, *Bonapartes in the New World*, p. 24; Philip Walsingham Sergeant, *Jérôme Bonaparte: The Burlesque Napoleon; Being the Story of the Life and Kingship of the Youngest Brother of Napoleon the Great* (Whitefish, Mont.: Kessinger, 2005), p. 75.

27 "a mere suspicion": Didier, *Life and Letters*, p. 20. For an excellent discussion of the political and cultural importance of fashion, see Charlotte Boyer Lewis, "Elizabeth Patterson Bonaparte: 'Ill Suited for the Life of a

Columbian's Modest Wife,' " *Journal of Women's History* 18, no. 2 (2006), pp. 33–62.

3 *"An Almost Naked Woman"*

28 "the agreeable Miss": See, for example, *Baltimore Federal Gazette,* December 27, 1803; *Commercial Advertiser* (New York), December 30, 1803; *Morning Chronicle* (New York), December 30, 1803; *New Jersey Journal* (Elizabeth Town), January 3, 1804; *Boston Gazette,* January 4, 1804.

28 After a brief stay: For a vivid description of the capital city, see Catherine Allgor, *Parlor Politics: In Which the Ladies of Washington Help to Build a City and a Government* (Charlottesville: University Press of Virginia, 2000), pp. 4–10.

29 Washington City: William Thomas Roberts Saffell, *The Bonaparte-Patterson Marriage in 1803* (General Books, 2009), p. 5; Helen Jean Burn, *Betsy Bonaparte* (Baltimore: Maryland Historical Society, 2010), p. 58; Geraldine Brooks, *Dames and Daughters of the Young Republic* (General Books, 2009), p. 59.

29 "Of Madame—I think": Mrs. Samuel Harrison Smith to Mrs. Kirkpatrick, January 23, 1804, in Gaillard Hunt, ed., *The First Forty Years of Washington Society, Portrayed by the Family Letters of Mrs. Samuel Harrison Smith (Margaret Bayard) from the Collection of Her Grandson, J. Henley Smith* (New York: Charles Scribner's Sons, 1906), pp. 44–47.

30 "you could see": Ibid.

30 "scarcely any waist": Rosalie Stier Calvert to Mme H. J. Stier, in Margaret Law Callcott, ed., *Mistress of Riversdale: The Plantation Letters of Rosalie Stier Calvert* (Baltimore: Johns Hopkins University Press, 1991), p. 78.

30 To her critics: Charlotte Boyer Lewis, "Elizabeth Patterson Bonaparte: 'Ill Suited for the Life of a Columbian's Modest Wife,' " *Journal of Women's History* 18, no. 2 (2006), pp. 33–62.

30 Betsy's embrace of Parisian: Jehanne Wake argues that a "rampant Gallomania" had seized other young American women. Jehanne Wake, *Sisters of Fortune: Marianne, Bess, Louisa, and Emily Caton, 1788–1874* (London: Chatto & Windus, 2010), p. 48.

31 "take a look at her bubbies": Carolyn Hoover Sung, "Catherine Mitchill's Letters from Washington, 1806–1812," *Quarterly Journal of the Library of Congress* 34 (July 1977), pp. 171–89, esp. pp. 182–84.

31 "Well! What of Madame Bonaparte": Ibid.

31 "if she did not change": Callcott, *Mistress of Riversdale,* p. 78; Claude Bourguignon-Frasseto, *Betsy Bonaparte: The Belle of Baltimore* (Baltimore: Maryland Historical Society, 2003), p. 43.

32 "a charming little woman": Aaron Burr to Theodosia Burr Alston, January 17, 1804, in Matthew L. Davis, ed., *Memoirs of Aaron Burr*, vol. 2 (Charleston, S.C.: Nabu Press, 2010), pp. 268–69.

32 "remarkable friendly": Sung, "Catherine Mitchill's Letters," pp. 182–84.

32 Betsy might have: See, for example, Betsy's annotations to James McIlhiny to EPB, September 5, 1815; James McIlhiny to EPB, January 16, 1817, MdHS, ms. 142; EPB to Mrs. M. H. Torres McCullugh, January 1861, MdHS, ms. 142; EPB's note on her father's will, n.d., MdHS, ms. 142.

33 Even if Betsy: Thomas Armstrong, *Politics, Diplomacy and Intrigue in the Early Republic: The Cabinet Career of Robert Smith, 1801–1811* (Dubuque, Ia.: Kendall Hunt, 1991), p. 10; Dorothy MacKay Quynn, "The Marriage of Betsy Patterson and Jérôme Bonaparte," unpublished ms., MdHS; Wake, *Sisters of Fortune*, p. 49; Gaillard Hunt, ed., *The First Forty Years of Washington Society*, pp. 44–47.

33 While Betsy and Jérôme: E. M. Oddie, *The Bonapartes in the New World* (London: Elkin Mathews and Marrot, 1932), p. 25; Quynn, "Marriage of Betsy Patterson," chap. 4.

34 "When we marry": Quoted in Eugène Lemoine Didier, *The Life and Letters of Madame Bonaparte* (Chestnut Hill, Mass.: Adamant Media, 2005, replica of 1879 edition), p. 23.

34 "I owe nothing": Clarence Edward McCartney and Gordon Dorrance, *The Bonapartes in America* (Philadelphia: Dorrance & Co., 1939), p. 24.

35 Napoleon's *Code Napoléon*: Sidney Mitchell, *A Family Lawsuit: The Romantic Story of Elisabeth Patterson and Jérôme Bonaparte* (New York: Farrar, Straus and Cudahy, 1958), p. 53.

35 "no more man": Oddie, *Bonapartes in the New World*, pp. 26–27.

35 William Patterson was not: Didier, *Life and Letters*, pp. 22–23.

35 The entire family: Mitchell, *Family Lawsuit*, pp. 49–50.

36 "young person with": Didier, *Life and Letters*, pp. 25, 28.

36 "a pretended marriage": Oddie, *Bonapartes in the New World*, p. 35.

36 But all this bad news: Mitchell, *Family Lawsuit*, p. 53.

37 "sole fabricator": Saffell, *Bonaparte-Patterson Marriage*, p. 23.

37 That September, Jérôme: For accounts of these efforts to sail for France, see Burn, *Betsy Bonaparte*, pp. 74–77; Didier, *Life and Letters*, pp. 21–22.

4 *"Have Confidence in Your Husband"*

40 "Tell your master": Eugène Lemoine Didier, *The Life and Letters of Madame Bonaparte* (Chestnut Hill, Mass.: Adamant Media, 2005, replica of 1879 edition), p. 37.

41 "Mon mari est": Quoted in Helen Jean Burn, *Betsy Bonaparte* (Baltimore: Maryland Historical Society, 2010), p. 85.

41 "the worst thing": Jérôme Bonaparte to EPB, April 8, 1805, MdHS, ms. 143.

42 "disposed to wash": William Thomas Roberts Saffell, *The Bonaparte-Patterson Marriage in 1803* (General Books, 2009), p. 98.

42 "So, sir, you are": Napoleon to Madame Mère, quoted in Sidney Mitchell, *A Family Lawsuit: The Romantic Story of Elisabeth Patterson and Jérôme Bonaparte* (New York: Farrar, Straus and Cudahy, 1958), pp. 65–66.

43 "She appears far": *Times* (London), May 19, 1805; Dorothy MacKay Quynn, "The Marriage of Betsy Patterson and Jérôme Bonaparte," unpublished ms., MdHS, chap. 7, n1.

44 "under the protection": *Times* (London), May 21, 1805.

44 Betsy surely appreciated: Mitchell, *Family Lawsuit*, p. 100.

45 "Would it be asking": EPB to Elisa Monroe, MdHS, ms. 142.

45 "Please let me know": Saffell, *Bonaparte-Patterson Marriage*, p. 210.

45 According to the doctor: Dr. Garnier to EPB, July 15, 1805, MdHS, ms. 142.

45 Betsy had no reason: Barbara Donegal to EPB, August 20, 1805, MdHS, ms. 142.

46 "Will you then": EPB to the Dowager Marchioness of Donegal, August 14, 1805, MdHS, ms. 142.

46 "Your daughter": Saffell, *Bonaparte-Patterson Marriage*, pp. 96, 98, 207–8.

47 "You know with what": Jérôme Bonaparte to EPB, July 29, 1805, MdHS, ms. 143.

48 This letter did not: M. Elgin to EPB, November 5, 1805; James McIlhiny to EPB, February 24, 1806, MdHS, ms. 142.

49 "sold to his own profit": Burn, *Betsy Bonaparte*, p. 115.

49 Betsy was enthusiastically: Jérôme Bonaparte to EPB, May 23, 1806, MdHS, ms. 143.

50 "Your departure for England": Jérôme Bonaparte to EPB, June 20, 1806, MdHS, ms. 143.

51 The king, who owed: Napoleon Bonaparte to Pope Pius VII, in Mitchell, *Family Lawsuit*, pp. 97, 98–99.

51 The pope was not persuaded: Pope Pius VII to Napoleon Bonaparte, June 27, 1805, ibid., pp. 109–11.

53 "that no one had the courage": Laure Junot Abrantès, *At the Court of Napoleon: Memoirs of the Duchesse d'Abrantès* (Gloucester, U.K.: Windrush Press, 1989), pp. 326, 329–30.

53 "I have seldom": J. M. Thompson, *Napoleon's Letters* (London: Prion, 1998), March 6, 1808.

54 "cares for nothing": Quoted in Clarence Edward McCartney and Gordon Dorrance, *The Bonapartes in America* (Philadelphia: Dorrance & Company, 1939).

5 *"Madame Bonaparte Is Ambitious"*

57 "speaks of you": Anna Kuhn to EPB, November 24. 1807, MdHS, ms. 142.

57 "It is a sign": Eliza Anderson to EPB, May 31, 1808, MdHS, ms. 142.

57 "dignity which I": Eliza Anderson to EPB, June 4, 1808, MdHS, ms. 142.

57 "splendidly provided for": Eliza Anderson to EPB, June 8, 1808, MdHS, ms. 142; see also Madame L. Breuil to EPB, June 20, 1810, MdHS, ms. 142.

58 On July 9: EPB to Turreau, July 8, 1808, MdHS, ms. 142.

58 Minister Turreau did: Notes on a letter from General Turreau, July 9, 1808, MdHS, ms. 142.

59 "Do not give in": Jérôme Bonaparte to EPB and William Patterson, May 16, 1808, MdHS, ms. 143.

59 Jérôme's conciliatory tone: Jérôme Bonaparte to EPB, November 22, 1808, MdHS, ms. 143.

60 "right to be": See EPB's annotation on Jérôme's letter of November 22, 1808, MdHS, ms. 143.

60 "I would rather": EPB to Prince Alexander Gorchakov, February 19, 1861, MdHS, ms. 142.

60 "be consigned to": EPB to James Monroe, October 15, 1808, MdHS, ms. 142.

61 "hard destiny which": James Monroe to EPB, November 6, 1808, MdHS, ms. 142.

61 "to accede to any offer": EPB to John Armstrong, March 17, 1809, MdHS, ms. 142.

62 "Tell Turreau that": Sidney Mitchell, *A Family Lawsuit: The Romantic Story of Elisabeth Patterson and Jérôme Bonaparte* (New York: Farrar, Straus and Cudahy, 1958), p. 167.

6 *"I Intend to Be Governed by My Own Rules"*

63 "most beautiful woman": Charlotte Boyer Lewis, "Elizabeth Patterson Bonaparte: 'Ill Suited for the Life of a Columbian's Modest Wife,'" *Journal of Women's History* 18, no. 2 (2006), pp. 33–62, esp. p. 42.

64 "When I first saw": Samuel Colleton Graves to EPB, May 16, 1808, MdHS, ms. 142.

65 "In returning": Samuel Colleton Graves to EPB, May 14, 1809, MdHS, ms. 142.

66 "I should extremely regret": EPB to Samuel Colleton Graves and Admiral Graves, May 16, 1809, MdHS, ms. 142.

66 "After the letter": Samuel Colleton Graves to EPB, July 27, 1809, MdHS, ms. 142.

67 "My husband & myself": Mrs. Graves to EPB, enclosure in Samuel Colleton Graves to EPB, July 27, 1809, MdHS, ms. 142.

67 "I feel regret at having": EPB to Mrs. Graves, December 1, 1809, MdHS, ms. 142.

68 "affectionate and devoted wife": "Marriage and Death Notices," *South Carolina Historical Magazine* 53, no. 3 (1952), p. 172.

68 Only a year before: See Spencer C. Tucker and Frank T. Reuter, *Injured Honor: The* Chesapeake-Leopard *Affair, June 22, 1807* (Annapolis: U.S. Naval Institute Press, 1996).

69 "Madame Bonaparte makes": Lydia Hollingsworth to her cousin, August 12, 1809, quoted in Helen Jean Burn, *Betsy Bonaparte* (Baltimore: Maryland Historical Society, 2010), p. 143.

69 "desperately in love": *Diary and Letters of Sir George Jackson, 1809–1816* (London, 1873), quoted in Dorothy MacKay Quynn, "The Marriage of Betsy Patterson and Jérôme Bonaparte," unpublished ms., MdHS.

70 Was Betsy using: See, for example, EPB to General John Armstrong, March 17, 1809, MdHS, ms. 142; Joseph Patterson to EPB, April 25, 1812, MdHS, ms. 142.

71 "to be governed": Claude Bourguignon-Frasseto, *Betsy Bonaparte: The Belle of Baltimore* (Baltimore: Maryland Historical Society, 2003), p. 106.

71 "I wonder how": Eliza Godefroy to EPB, 1809, MdHS, ms. 142.

7 *"I Shall Resume the Name of My Own Family"*

72 Writing to Dolley: EPB to Dolley Payne Todd Madison, November 22, 1813, in Holly C. Shulman, ed., *The Dolley Madison Digital Edition,* http://rotunda.upress.virginia.edu/dmde.

73 "No novelties here": EPB to Mr. Willink, March 2, 1812, MdHS, ms. 142.

73 "The more I see": Elbridge Gerry to Ann Gerry, July 3, 1813, in *Proceedings of the Massachusetts Historical Society* 47, 3rd series (October 1913–June 1914), pp. 445–534.

73 Despite her best efforts: See Eliza Anderson [Godefroy] to EPB, May 31, 1808, MdHS, ms. 142.

75 "a Court, which in splendor": Charlene Boyer Lewis, "Elizabeth Pat-

terson Bonaparte: 'Ill Suited for the Life of a Columbian's Modest Wife,'" *Journal of Women's History* 18, no. 2 (2006), pp. 45–46; Charlene Boyer Lewis, "Elizabeth Patterson Bonaparte: A Woman Between Two Worlds," in Leonard J. Sadosky et al., eds., *Old World, New World: America and Europe in the Age of Jefferson* (Charlottesville: University of Virginia Press, 2010), p. 258.

75 By the end of 1811: John Purviance to EPB, July 16, 1811; EPB to Mr. Servier [Serurier], July 8, 1811; Lescailier to EPB, October 7, 1811; EPB to Lescalier, October 10, 1811; all in MdHS, ms. 142.

76 For in the very year: Jérôme Bonaparte to EPB and Jerome Napoleon Bonaparte [hereafter Bo], February 20, 1812, MdHS, ms. 143.

76 After being reassured: Joseph Patterson to EPB, April 25, 1812, MdHS, ms. 142.

77 "an act annulling": Archives of Maryland Online, Sessions Laws, 1812, vol. 618, p. 145

77 "hurled me back": EPB to Sydney Morgan, March 14, 1849, in William Hepworth Dixon, ed., *Lady Morgan Memoirs: Autobiography, Diaries and Correspondence*, 2nd ed. (London, 1863), pp. 2:502–4. See also EPB to editors of *The New American Cyclopaedia*, n.d. c. 1852, MdHS, ms. 142; EPB to Alexander Gorchakov, February 19, 1861, MdHS, ms. 142.

78 "The obstacles which": EPB to Dolley Payne Todd Madison, December 29, 1814; Dolley Payne Todd Madison to EPB, December 31, 1814, both in Shulman, *Dolley Madison Digital Edition.*

79 "was very sick": Caroline Patterson to EPB, January 1814, MdHS, ms. 142. For Betsy's resentment of her father's infidelity, see, for example, her annotations to James McIlhiny to EPB, August 29, 1815, September 5, 1815, and January 16, 1817, MdHS, ms. 142.

80 "This scheme requires": Lydia Hollingsworth to Ruth Tobin, March 27, 1815, quoted in Helen Jean Burn, *Betsy Bonaparte* (Baltimore: Maryland Historical Society, 2010), p. 166.

8 *"The Purposes of Life Are All Fulfilled"*

81 "O Turn thou": William Johnson to EPB, March 28, 1814, MdHS, ms. 142.

81 Betsy had prepared: EPB to Thomas Jefferson, March 25, 1815, Thomas Jefferson Papers, Library of Congress.

81 Jefferson feared that: Thomas Jefferson to EPB, April 24, 1815, Thomas Jefferson Papers, Library of Congress.

81 But Betsy's uncle: Samuel Smith to Lafayette, April 18, 1815, MdHS, ms. 142.

81 Richard Gilmore sent: Richard Gilmore to Madame Licama, April 10, 1815, and Richard Gilmore to Madame Schimmelpennick, April 10, 1815, MdHS, ms. 142.

82 And Jan Willink: John A. Willink to William Willink, April 17, 1815, MdHS, ms. 142.

82 "conceived a residence": James McIlhiny to EPB, August 29, 1815, including EPB's annotation, MdHS, ms. 142; see also EPB's annotation to six McIlhiny letters, c. 1861, MdHS, ms. 142.

83 "so particular about": Claude Bourguignon-Frasseto, *Betsy Bonaparte: The Belle of Baltimore* (Baltimore: Maryland Historical Society, 2003), pp. 123, 128–29; E. M. Oddie, *The Bonapartes in the New World* (London: Elkin Mathews and Marrot, 1932), pp. 73–79; Helen Jean Burn, *Betsy Bonaparte* (Baltimore: Maryland Historical Society, 2010), p. 169.

84 "cherished, visited": Bourguignon-Frasseto, *Betsy Bonaparte*, p. 127.

84 "Europe more than": EPB to William Patterson, September 23, 1815, in Eugène Lemoine Didier, *The Life and Letters of Madame Bonaparte* (Chestnut Hill, Mass.: Adamant Media, 2005, replica of 1879 edition), pp. 61–62.

84 "I am convinced": William Patterson to EPB, November 16, December 15, 1815, MdHS, ms. 145.

85 "I fear it may give": James McIlhiny to EPB, September 5, 1815, MdHS, ms. 142.

85 "It was with the most": Edward Patterson to EPB, November 16, 1815, MdHS, ms. 142.

86 "the same old": John Spear Smith to EPB, November 18, 1815, MdHS, ms. 142.

86 "I think it both wicked": Ann "Nancy" Spear to EPB, December 1, 1815, MdHS, ms. 142.

86 "tales allegedly spread": Mary Mansfield to EPB, December 27, 1815, MdHS, ms. 142.

86 "Health Character attention": EPB annotation, James McIlhiny to EPB, September 5, 1815, MdHS, ms. 142.

86 "This will find you": Edward Patterson to EPB, December 15, 1815, MdHS, ms. 142.

87 "It appears to me": Didier, *Life and Letters,* pp. 54–58.

87 "consider me an apostate": EPB to [John Spear Smith], August 22, 1816, MdHS, ms. 142.

88 William did not understand: Didier, *Life and Letters,* pp. 62–63.

89 "Satisf[y] her curiosity": James McIlhiny to EPB, n.d. 1816, MdHS, ms. 142.

89 "Mr Patterson's objection": EPB annotation to James McIlhiny, n.d. 1816, MdHS, ms. 142.

90 "Everyone who knows me": Didier, *Life and Letters,* pp. 54–58.

90 "the Conquerer of": Eliza Godefroy to EPB, March 17, 1816, MdHS, ms. 142.

91 "In my dreams": EPB to Mary Caton Patterson, November 7, 1815, quoted in Burn, *Betsy Bonaparte,* p. 173.

92 "The Plague sore": Ann "Nancy" Spear to EPB, January 14, 1816, May 1, 1816, May 30, 1816, MdHS, ms. 142.

9 "Your Ideas Soar'd Too High"

93 All Paris did: Eugène Lemoine Didier, *The Life and Letters of Madame Bonaparte* (Chestnut Hill, Mass.: Adamant Media, 2005, replica of 1879 edition), pp. 63–64.

93 "It is now generally reported": John Spear Smith to EPB, April 18–May 25, 1816, MdHS, ms. 142.

93 "You must certainly": Ann "Nancy" Spear to EPB, May 30, 1816, MdHS, ms. 142.

94 It was true that lovesick: Claude Bourguignon-Frasseto, *Betsy Bonaparte: The Belle of Baltimore* (Baltimore: Maryland Historical Society, 2003), p. 149.

94 "for some weeks": EPB to John Spear Smith, August 22, 1816, MdHS, ms. 142.

95 Those invitations came: Amelia Ruth Gere Mason, *The Women of the French Salons* (New York: Century, 1891), pp. 69, 128.

95 "If I were a queen": EPB to Sydney Morgan, November 28, 1816, in William Hepworth Dixon, ed., *Lady Morgan Memoirs: Autobiography, Diaries and Correspondence,* 2nd ed. (London, 1863), pp. 45–47; Mason, *Women of the French Salons,* p. 138; Helen Jean Burn, *Betsy Bonaparte* (Baltimore: Maryland Historical Society, 2010), pp. 175–76.

96 Warden also introduced: Mason, *Women of the Salons,* pp. 148–51.

96 Sydney's literary talents: Dixon, *Lady Morgan Memoirs,* introduction.

97 Over her lifetime: EPB to Sydney Morgan, September 23, 1816, November 18, 1816, September 30, 1820, September 22, 1839, March 14, 1849, in Dixon, *Lady Morgan Memoirs,* pp. 42–44, 45–47, 62–65, 140–42, 454–56, 502–4.

97 "their whining": EPB to John Spear Smith, August 22, 1816, MdHS, ms. 142.

98 "where no pleasures": Ibid.

99 "those long wearisome": Ibid.
99 "shut up in our melancholy": Ibid.
99 "tone of tristesse": Sydney Morgan to EPB, May 26, 1817, MdHS, ms. 142.
101 "an Eroneous": James McIlhiny to EPB, September 18, 1817, MdHS, ms. 142.

10 *"For This Life There Is Nothing but Disappointment"*

101 Betsy understood both: EPB to Sydney Morgan, May 23, 1818, in William Hepworth Dixon, ed., *Lady Morgan Memoirs: Autobiography, Diaries and Correspondence,* 2nd ed. (London, 1863), pp. 80–84; for letters dealing with finances see, for example, Edward Patterson to EPB, September 20, September 25, 1816, March 14, 1817, in MdHS, ms. 142; EPB to William Patterson, September 19, 1821, in Eugène Lemoine Didier, *The Life and Letters of Madame Bonaparte* (Chestnut Hill, Mass.: Adamant Media, 2005, replica of 1879 edition), pp. 89–90; EPB to Eliza Patterson, March 14, 1817, MdHS, ms. 142.

102 Betsy was probably: EPB to Sydney Morgan, October 1, 1819, in Dixon, *Lady Morgan Memoirs,* pp. 108–11.

103 William, in turn: William Patterson to EPB, April 23, 1827, MdHS, ms. 145.

104 "I shall hasten": Didier, *Life and Letters,* p. 86.

104 Bo's longing for home: Bo to William Patterson, November 6, 1820, in Didier, *Life and Letters,* pp. 75–77; Helen Jean Burn, *Betsy Bonaparte* (Baltimore: Maryland Historical Society, 2010), p. 75.

105 "Mamma goes out": Didier, *Life and Letters,* p. 85.

105 "She says she looks": Ibid., p. 86; Charlotte Boyer Lewis, "Elizabeth Patterson Bonaparte: 'Ill Suited for the Life of a Columbian's Modest Wife,'" *Journal of Women's History* 18, no. 2 (2006), p. 50.

106 "I was not surprised": Virginia Tatnall Peacock, *Famous American Belles of the Nineteenth Century* (Books for Libraries Press, n.d., reissued by University, 2011), p. 57; Clarence Edward McCartney and Gordon Dorrance, *The Bonapartes in America* (Philadelphia: Dorrance & Co., 1939), p. 37.

106 "He seems, poor man": Axel Madsen, *John Jacob Astor, America's First Multimillionaire* (New York: John Wiley & Sons, 2001); Burn, *Betsy Bonaparte,* p. 187.

106 In the autumn of 1819: John Jacob Astor to EPB, April 23, 1820, MdHS, ms. 142.

107 In March 1820: EPB to William Patterson, May 8, 1820, in Didier, *Life and Letters,* pp. 80–82; Claude Bourguignon-Frasseto, *Betsy Bonaparte:*

The Belle of Baltimore (Baltimore: Maryland Historical Society, 2003), pp. 168–69.

108 "If I took my son": EPB to William Patterson, April 10, 1820, in Didier, *Life and Letters,* pp. 66–70.

108 "necessity of application": Ibid.

108 "without an education": Ibid.

109 In a letter to Pauline: EPB to Princess [Pauline Bonaparte] Borghese, March 25, 1820, in Didier, *Life and Letters,* pp. 70–72.

109 "spends everything he can": EPB to William Patterson, April 25, 1820, ibid., pp. 74–77.

111 Pauline seemed equally: EPB to William Patterson, November 28, 1821, ibid., pp. 93–96; Flora Fraser, *Pauline Bonaparte: Venus of Empire* (New York: Knopf, 2009), pp. 227–37.

112 Joseph Bonaparte was: Patricia Tyson Stroud, *The Man Who Had Been King: The American Exile of Napoleon's Brother Joseph* (Philadelphia: University of Pennsylvania Press, 2005).

113 "entirely ruined, his fortune": EPB to William Patterson, November 28, 1821, in Didier, *Life and Letters,* pp. 93–96.

113 "Since I have been": Bo to William Patterson, n.d., ibid., p. 86.

114 "There is no knowing": EPB to William Patterson, January 29–30, 1822, ibid., pp. 102–5.

114 "discourage all that tendency": EPB to William Patterson, March 8, 1822, ibid., pp. 108–9.

114 "exactly as she has done": EPB to William Patterson, January 29–30, 1822, ibid., pp. 102–5.

115 "are those who support": EPB to William Patterson, December 21, 1821, ibid., pp. 96–97.

115 "It is generally": EPB to William Patterson, October 16, 1821, ibid., pp. 90–92.

11 *"That Was My American Wife"*

116 "You may not have reigned": Claude Bourguignon-Frasseto, *Betsy Bonaparte: The Belle of Baltimore* (Baltimore: Maryland Historical Society, 2003), p. 172.

117 "Did you see?": There are several slightly different accounts of this meeting. See, for example, Eugène Lemoine Didier, *The Life and Letters of Madame Bonaparte* (Chestnut Hill, Mass.: Adamant Media, 2005, replica of 1879 edition), p. 113; Virginia Tatnall Peacock, *Famous American Belles of the Nineteenth Century* (Books for Libraries Press, n.d., reis-

sued by University, 2011), p. 57; Bourguignon-Frasseto, *Betsy Bonaparte,* p. 192.

117 That enduring beauty: Ann "Nancy" Spear to EPB, April 12, 1827, MdHS, ms. 142.

117 "the extreme profligacy": Earl of Ilchester, ed., *The Journal of the Hon. Henry Edward Fox, 1818–1830* (London: Thornton Butterworth, 1932), p. 319.

117 "I every Day miss": Sir George Dallas to [Lady Dallas], December 13, 1827, MdHS, ms. 142.

118 "The land of romance": See, for example, EPB to William Patterson, July 7, 1822, February 5, 1923, November 9, 1823, in Didier, *Life and Letters,* pp. 113–16, 134–35, 159–60.

118 "the next best thing": EPB to William Patterson, December 4, 1829, ibid., pp. 231–32.

120 "We must instill ambition": EPB to William Patterson, July 7, 1822, ibid., pp. 113–16.

120 "Disappointments," she wrote: EPB to William Patterson, December 24, 1822, February 15, 1823, ibid., pp. 126–26, 139–41.

121 "young people are often": EPB to William Patterson, October 15, December 11, 1822, ibid., pp. 124, 125.

121 Thus far Betsy: EPB to William Patterson, December 24–27, 1822, in Dorothy MacKay Quynn, "The Marriage of Betsy Patterson and Jérôme Bonaparte," unpublished ms., MdHS, p. 17.

121 "However advantageous": Bo to William Patterson, March 3, 1824, in Didier, *Life and Letters,* pp. 166–67.

122 Although Bo's extravagance: Bo to William Patterson, August 16, 1824, ibid., pp. 168–69.

123 When Bo returned: William Patterson to EPB, September 14, 1824, MdHS, ms. 145.

123 "I have no confidence": EPB to William Patterson, July 7, 1822, May 22, 1823, in Didier, *Life and Letters,* pp. 113–16, 152–54.

124 No matter how: EPB to Sydney Morgan, n.d., ibid., pp. 171–73.

124 Betsy arrived at Le Havre: EPB to Sydney Morgan, November 28, 1825, ibid., pp. 184–85.

125 "*mere* adventurers": Jehanne Wake, *Sisters of Fortune: Marianne, Bess, Louisa, and Emily Caton, 1788–1874* (London: Chatto & Windus, 2010), esp. p. 189; EPB to William Patterson, November 2, 1825, in Didier, *Life and Letters,* pp. 181–83.

125 "I should pass": EPB to William Patterson, February 21, 1826, in Didier, *Life and Letters,* pp. 188–89.

126 "My dear child," he wrote: Jérôme Bonaparte to Bo, March 6, 1826, ibid., pp. 190–91.

127 "I have seen a great": Bo to William Patterson, n.d., 1826, ibid., pp. 195–96.

127 "I perceive that he": William Patterson to EPB, April 23, 1827, MdHS, ms. 145.

127 "You seem somewhat angry": Ibid.

129 "I am excessively tired": Bo to William Patterson, January 7, January 25, 1827, in Didier, *Life and Letters,* pp. 210, 211–12.

129 "think of doing something": Bo to William Patterson, January 25, 1827, ibid., pp. 211–21.

12 *"He Has Neither My Pride, My Ambition, nor My Love of Good Company"*

130 "Your father's family": William Patterson to Bo, August 14, 1825, in Eugène Lemoine Didier, *The Life and Letters of Madame Bonaparte* (Chestnut Hill, Mass.: Adamant Media, 2005, replica of 1879 edition), pp. 176–77.

131 The only stumbling block: William Patterson to EPB, July 24, November 4, 1829, MdHS, ms. 145.

131 "determined not to marry": William Patterson to EPB, July 24, 1829, MdHS, ms. 145.

132 Still Betsy was kept: EPB to William Patterson, May 30, 1828, in Didier, *Life and Letters,* pp. 221–23.

132 "If he were a Minor": EPB to William Patterson, September 9, October 17, 1829, MdHS, ms. 145.

133 Betsy's suspicions: William Patterson to EPB, November 4, 1829, MdHS, ms. 145; Edward Patterson to EPB, October 27, 1829, March 30, 1830, MdHS, ms. 142.

133 "look back on": William Patterson to EPB, November 4, 1829, MdHS, ms. 145.

134 "I think that": EPB to William Patterson, December 4, 1829, in Didier, *Life and Letters,* pp. 231–32.

134 "Please Understand, Maman": Quoted in Claude Bourguignon-Frasseto, *Betsy Bonaparte: The Belle of Baltimore* (Baltimore: Maryland Historical Society, 2003), p. 206.

135 "by nature rather indolent": Edward Patterson to EPB, March 5 1830, MdHS, ms. 142.

135 "I have gained": EPB to William Patterson, December 21, 1829, in Didier, *Life and Letters,* pp. 233–34.

136 "A duller person": Quoted in Helen Jean Burn, *Betsy Bonaparte* (Baltimore: Maryland Historical Society, 2010), p. 207.

136 Betsy's attraction to Gorchakov: See Dorothy MacKay Quynn, "The Marriage of Betsy Patterson and Jérôme Bonaparte," unpublished ms., MdHS; "Portrait of Prince Gorchakoff," MdHS, ms. 142; Burn, *Betsy Bonaparte,* pp. 206–8; Bourguignon-Frasseto, *Betsy Bonaparte,* pp. 240–41.

13 *"Disgusted with the Past, Despairing of a Future"*

139 "Every thing is turning": William Patterson to EPB, November 27, 1830, MdHS, ms. 145.

140 "Let them all descend": EPB to John White, August 20, 1833, MdHS, ms. 145; Dorothy MacKay Quynn, "The Marriage of Betsy Patterson and Jérôme Bonaparte," unpublished ms., MdHS, chap. 13, p. 26.

141 "We are in great confusion": William Patterson to EPB, March 10, 1834, MdHS, ms. 145.

141 "sweet home": Ibid.

141 "Your father is excessively": Ann "Nancy" Spear to EPB, August 4, 1833, MdHS, ms. 142.

142 "How could you": William Patterson to EPB, March 10, 1834, MdHS, ms. 145.

143 "The conduct of": See William Patterson's Will, MdHS, ms. 145; Dorothy MacKay Quynn, "The Truth About Betsy Patterson," May 1953, unpublished ms., MdHS, ms. 2194; Eugène Lemoine Didier, *The Life and Letters of Madame Bonaparte* (Chestnut Hill, Mass.: Adamant Media, 2005, replica of 1879 edition), pp. 256–57.

143 "The clause in his will": EPB, notes on her father's will, n.d., MdHS, ms. 142.

145 At William's death: William Patterson's Will, MdHS, ms. 145.

147 They had found: John Patterson to EPB, February 15 1835, MdHS, ms. 142; Roger Taney to John Sergeant and Horace Birney, May 6, 1835, MDHS, ms. 142; Helen Jean Burn, *Betsy Bonaparte* (Baltimore: Maryland Historical Society, 2010), pp. 212–16.

148 "graphic description": EPB to George Patterson, August 12, 1835, MdHS, ms. 142

148 "Edward loved me,": Burn, *Betsy Bonaparte,* p. 216.

148 "Having told many": EPB to George Patterson, August 12, 1835, MdHS, ms. 142.

148 "Quaint Companion": Poem, MdHS, ms. 142.

149 "He never says": Note in EPB's hand on letter from Bo to EPB, March 31, 1835, MdHS, ms. 142.

149 "no one who has": EPB to William Patterson, February 12, 1827, in Didier, *Life and Letters,* pp. 213–15; Burn, *Betsy Bonaparte,* p. 219.

14 "My Birth Is Legitimate"

150 "melancholy and regrets": EPB to Sydney Morgan, September 22, 1839, in William Hepworth Dixon, ed., *Lady Morgan Memoirs: Autobiography, Diaries and Correspondence,* 2nd ed. (London, 1863), pp. 454–56.

150 Bo too had come to Europe: EPB to Sydney Morgan, September 22, 1839, ibid., pp. 454–56.

151 Here her life took: Eugène Lemoine Didier, *The Life and Letters of Madame Bonaparte* (Chestnut Hill, Mass.: Adamant Media, 2005, replica of 1879 edition), pp. 261–62.

152 "I do feel enchanted": EPB to Sydney Morgan, March 14, 1849, in Dixon, *Lady Morgan Memoirs,* pp. 222–23; Sidney Mitchell, *A Family Lawsuit: The Romantic Story of Elisabeth Patterson and Jérôme Bonaparte* (New York: Farrar, Straus and Cudahy, 1958), p. 143.

152 While Betsy and Sydney: See John Bierman, *Napoleon III and His Carnival Empire* (New York: St. Martin's Press, 1988).

153 "I only wish that": EPB to James Gallatin, May 4, and November 3, 1852, MdHS, ms. 142.

154 "I have never coveted": EPB to editors of *The New American Cyclopaedia,* n.d. [1852], MdHS, ms. 142.

154 "received with great pleasure": Bo to Napoleon III, January 1, 1853; Napoleon III to Bo, February 9, 1853, MdHS, ms. 144; Didier, *Life and Letters,* p. 267.

155 Bo took the emperor's words: Mitchell, *Family Lawsuit,* pp. 143–45.

155 More signs of favor: Ibid., pp. 145–46.

155 At first this reunion: Philip Walsingham Sergeant, *Jérôme Bonaparte: The Burlesque Napoleon; Being the Story of the Life and Kingship of the Youngest Brother of Napoleon the Great* (Whitefish, Mont.: Kessinger, 2005), p. 373.

156 "The most prodigiously": Helen Jean Burn, *Betsy Bonaparte* (Baltimore: Maryland Historical Society, 2010), p. 229; Mitchell, *Family Lawsuit,* p. 146.

157 "In the event that we should leave": E. M. Oddie, *The Bonapartes in the New World* (London: Elkin Mathews and Marrot, 1932), pp. 209–10.

158 "addressed to him": Mitchell, *Family Lawsuit,* p. 147n. The prince impe-

rial, Napoleon Eugène Louis Jean Joseph Bonaparte, was born in March 1856 and would be killed in battle in Africa in June 1879.

158 In the decision: Mitchell, *Family Lawsuit,* pp. 148–51; Didier, *Life and Letters,* p. 270.

158 "Since no man creates": Mitchell, *Family Lawsuit,* pp. 151–52.

159 Before leaving France: Ibid., p. 153n.

159 Betsy was cruelly: See, for example, *Daily National Intelligencer* (Washington, D.C.); *New Hampshire Statesman,* December 25, 1852; *Daily Morning News* (Savannah, Ga.), July 26, 1856; *New York Herald,* August 9, 1856; *Newark Advocate* (Newark, Ohio), September 17, 1856.

160 "to ascertain, vindicate": EPB to Berryer, October 13, 1858; EPB to Alexander Gorchakov, ca. 1858, MdHS, ms. 142; See letters between EPB and Berryer, December 1857–January 1859, MdHS, ms. 142.

160 "His death creates": *Daily Sentinel* (Milwaukee), July 16, 1860.

160 "His first wife": *Harper's Weekly,* July 28, 1860.

15 "I Will Never Be Dupe Enough Ever to Try Justice in France"

162 Fort Sumter: *Harper's Weekly,* March 9, 1861; New York *Herald,* February 11, February 16, 1861; *Boston Daily Advertiser,* May 9, 1861; *New Hampshire Statesman,* October 5, 1866.

162 "My time," Betsy had written: EPB to John White, February 11, 1861, printed in *The Collector: A Magazine for Autograph & Historical Collectors,* December 1956, in MdHS.

163 "I am for life": Bo to Jerome Napoleon Bonaparte, September 5, 1840, in Sidney Mitchell, *A Family Lawsuit: The Romantic Story of Elisabeth Patterson and Jérôme Bonaparte* (New York: Farrar, Straus and Cudahy, 1958), p. 139.

163 Just as the battle: Helen Jean Burn, *Betsy Bonaparte* (Baltimore: Maryland Historical Society, 2010), p. 235.

164 "I am confident": Junior to Bo, July 11, 1860, MdHS, ms. 144.

165 "the children of a second marriage": Mitchell, *Family Lawsuit,* pp. 77–153; E. M. Oddie, *The Bonapartes in the New World* (London: Elkin Mathews and Marrot, 1932), pp. 231–32.

167 Betsy, he continued: Mitchell, *Family Lawsuit,* pp. 77–153; Burn, *Betsy Bonaparte,* pp. 236–39.

167 In a long letter: EPB to Alexander Gorchakov, February 19, 1861, MdHS, ms. 142.

167 "personage, whose poverty": Ibid.

168 "This drop in eternity": Ibid.

169 "in order and": Mitchell, *Family Lawsuit,* pp. 158–59.

169 "with Philosophy, resignation": EPB to Lady Westmoreland, n.d., MdHS, ms. 142.

169 "to follow my example": Mitchell, *Family Lawsuit,* pp. 196–97.

170 "I will never be dupe": EPB to Bo, July 18, 1861, MdHS, ms. 142.

170 Betsy's confidence: See, for example, *Examiner* (London), February 16, 1861; *Athenaeum* (London), August 31, 1861; *New York Herald,* February 16, 1861.

171 "fool and a poltroon": *Athenaeum* (London), August 31, 1861.

16 *"Once I Had Everything but Money; Now I Have Nothing but Money"*

173 "I can tell you nothing": EPB to Mr. Guillardet, April 19, 1964, MdHS, ms. 142.

174 Betsy was determined: Helen Jean Burn, *Betsy Bonaparte* (Baltimore: Maryland Historical Society, 2010), p. 243.

174 "Once I had everything": Quoted in Eugène Lemoine Didier, *The Life and Letters of Madame Bonaparte* (Chestnut Hill, Mass.: Adamant Media, 2005, replica of 1879 edition), p. 274.

175 Her present condition: William Thomas Roberts Saffell, *The Bonaparte-Patterson Marriage in 1803* (General Books, 2009), p. 233.

175 "retains TRACES": Quoting an article in *Baltimore Sun,* January 19, 1870.

175 "an unknown Madman": John Prichard to EPB, October 9, 1869, February 1872, May 1872, MdHS, ms. 142.

175 beautiful blue eyes: John Perkergrue to EPB, ca. 1872, MdHS, ms. 142.

175 Charley, now in his twenties: For a biography of Charles Bonaparte, see Joseph Bucklin Bishop, *Charles Joseph Bonaparte: His Life and Public Services* (New York: Charles Scribner's Sons, 1922).

176 "The humiliating Shame": EPB to Junior, August 18, 1871, MdHS, ms. 142.

177 "filled with astonishment": Ibid.

177 She engaged in battles: The *Dialogue* is lost.

178 "Her nature is suspicious": Saffell, *Bonaparte-Patterson Marriage,* p. 233; Didier, *Life and Letters,* pp. 274, 277–78.

179 "She passed away quietly": Didier, *Life and Letters,* pp. 277–80.

Conclusion *"I Have Lived Alone and I Will Die Alone"*

188 "I have lived": Quoted in Helen Jean Burn, *Betsy Bonaparte* (Baltimore: Maryland Historical Society, 2010), p. 246.

Epilogue *The American Bonapartes*

192 "an honest-to-goodness": This and following quotes from "Charles J. Bonaparte, Founder of the FBI," Italian Historical Society of America, accessed October 8, 2013, http://www.italianhistorical.org/page61.html.

Bibliography

Primary Sources

Archives of Maryland, Sessions Laws, 1812
Elizabeth Patterson Bonaparte Papers, Maryland Historical Society
Jerome Bonaparte Papers, Maryland Historical Society
William Patterson Papers, Maryland History Society
Jerome Napoleon Bonaparte Papers, Maryland Historical Society
Elbridge Gerry Papers, Massachusetts Historical Society
Papers of Dolley Madison, Digital Edition, ed. Holly C. Shulman

Books

Abrantes, Laure Junot. *At the Court of Napoleon: Memoirs of the Duchesse d'Abrantes.* Gloucestershire, U.K.: Windrush Press, 1991.

Allgor, Catherine. *Parlor Politics: In Which the Ladies of Washington Help Build a City and a Government.* Charlottesville and London: University of Virginia Press, 2000.

Armstrong, Thomas. *The Cabinet Career of Robert Smith, 1801–1811.* Dubuque, Iowa: Kendall Hunt Publishing Company, 1991.

———. *Politics, Diplomacy, and Intrigue in the Early Republic.* Dubuque, Iowa: Kendall Hunt Publishing Company, 1992.

Beirne, Francis F. *The Amiable Baltimoreans.* Baltimore: Johns Hopkins University Press, 1984.

Bierman, John. *Napoleon III and His Carnival Empire.* New York: St. Martin's Press, 1988.

Bishop, Joseph Bucklin. *Charles Joseph Bonaparte: His Life and Public Services.* New York: Charles Scribner's Sons, 1922.

Bourguignon-Frasseto, Claude. *Betsy Bonaparte: The Belle of Baltimore.* Baltimore: Maryland Historical Society, 2003.

Brooks, Geraldine. *Dames and Daughters of the Young Republic.* General Books, 2009.

Burn, Helen Jean. *Betsy Bonaparte*. Baltimore: Maryland Historical Society, 2010.

Callcott, Margaret Law, ed. *Mistress of Riversdale: The Plantation Letters of Rosalie Stier Calvert, 1795–1821*. Baltimore: Johns Hopkins University Press, 1992.

Davis, Matthew L. *Memoirs of Aaron Burr*, vol. 2. Charleston, S.C.: Nabu Press, 2010.

Davis, Richard Beale, ed. [Sir August John Foster, Bart.] *Jefferson's America: Notes on the United States of America*. San Marino, Calif.: Huntington Library, 1954.

Didier, Eugene Lemoine. *The Life and Letters of Madame Bonaparte*. Chestnut Hill, Mass.: Adamant Media Corporation, 2005; replica of 1879 edition, Sampson Low, Marston, Searle & Rivington, London.

Dixon, William Hepworth, ed. *Lady Morgan Memoirs: Autobiography, Diaries and Correspondence*, vol. 2. 2nd ed., London, 1863.

Ford, Paul Leicester, ed. *The Works of Thomas Jefferson in Twelve Volumes*. Vol. 10, *Correspondence and Papers, 1803–1807*. New York: G. P. Putnam's Sons, 1904–5.

Foreman, Amanda. *Georgiana: Duchess of Devonshire*. New York: Random House, 2000.

Fraser, Flora. *Pauline Bonaparte: Venus of Empire*. New York: Knopf, 2009.

Goodman, Dena. *The Republic of Letters: A Cultural History of the French Enlightenment*. Ithaca, N.Y.: Cornell University Press, 1996.

Howland, Richard Hubbard. *The Architecture of Baltimore*. Baltimore: Johns Hopkins University Press, 1953.

Hunt, Gaillard, ed. *The First Forty Years of Washington Society, Portrayed by the Family Letters of Mrs. Samuel Harrison Smith (Margaret Bayard) from the Collection of Her Grandson, J. Henley Smith*. New York: Charles Scribner's Sons, 1906.

Earl of Ilchester, ed. *The Journal of the Hon. Henry Edward Fox, 1818–1830*. London: Butterworth, 1923.

Jackson, Sir George. *Diary and Letters of Sir George Jackson, 1809–1816*. London, 1873, 2 vols.

Kale, Steven. *French Salons: High Society and Political Stability from the Old Regime to the Revolution of 1848*. Baltimore: Johns Hopkins University Press, 2004.

Kircheisen, F. M. *Memoirs of Napoleon the First. Compiled from His Writings*. New York: Duffield & Company, 1929.

Madson, Axel. *John Jacob Astor: America's First Multimillionaire*. New York: Wiley, 2001.

Mason, Amelia Ruth Gere. *The Women of the French Salons.* New York: Century, 1891.

McCartney, Clarence Edward, and Gordon Dorrance. *The Bonapartes in America.* Philadelphia: Dorrance & Company, 1939.

Mitchell, Sidney. *A Family Lawsuit: The Romantic Story of Elisabeth Patterson and Jerome Bonaparte.* New York: Farrar, Straus and Cudahy, 1958.

Oddie, E. M. *The Bonapartes in the New World.* London: Elkin Mathews and Marrot, 1932.

Pancake, John. *Samuel Smith and the Politics of Business, 1782–1839.* Tuscaloosa: University of Alabama Press, 1972.

Peacock, Virginia Tatnall. *Famous American Belles of the Nineteenth Century.* Freeport, N.Y.: Books for Libraries Press. Reissued, University, 2011.

Saffell, William Thomas Roberts. *The Bonaparte-Patterson Marriage in 1803.* General Books, 2009.

Sergeant, Philip Walsingham. *Jerome Bonaparte: The Burlesque Napoleon; Being the Story of the Life and Kingship of the Youngest Brother of Napoleon the Great.* Whitefish, Mont.: Kessinger Publishing, 2005.

Sioussat, Annie Leakin. *Old Baltimore.* New York: Macmillan & Company, 1931.

Stowe, William W. *Going Abroad: European Travel in Nineteenth Century American Culture.* Princeton, N.J.: Princeton University Press, 1994.

Stroud, Patricia Tyson. *The Emperor of Nature: Charles-Lucien Bonaparte and His World.* Philadelphia: University of Pennsylvania Press, 2000.

———. *The Man Who Had Been King: The American Exile of Napoleon's Brother Joseph.* Philadelphia: University of Pennsylvania Press, 2005.

Tucker, Spencer C., and Frank T. Reuter. *Injured Honor: The Chesapeake-Leopard Affair, June 22, 1807.* Annapolis, Md.: U.S. Naval Institute Press, 1996.

Wake, Jehanne. *Sisters of Fortune: Marianne, Bess, Louisa, and Emily Caton, 1788–1874.* London: Chatto & Windus, 2010.

Articles

Kilbride, Daniel. "Travel, Ritual, and National Identity: Planters on the European Tour, 1820–1860." *The Journal of Southern History* 69, no. 3 (August 2003), 549–84.

Lewis, Charlene Boyer. "Elizabeth Patterson Bonaparte: 'Ill Suited for the Life of a Columbian's Modest Wife." *Journal of Women's History* 18, no. 2 (2006), 33–62.

———. "Elizabeth Patterson Bonaparte: A Woman Between Two Worlds," in L. Sadosky et al., *Old World, New World: America and Europe in the Age of Jefferson.* Charlottesville: University of Virginia Press, 2010.

Quynn, Dorothy MacKay. "The Marriage of Betsy Bonaparte and Jerome Bonaparte." Unpublished manuscript, Maryland Historical Society.

————. "The Truth About Betsy Patterson." May 1953. Unpublished manuscript, Maryland Historical Society.

Sung, Carolyn Hoover. "Catherine Mitchill's Letters from Washington, 1806–1812," *Quarterly Journal of the Library of Congress* 34 (July 1977), 182–84.

Index

A Note on the Type

This book was set in Adobe Garamond. Designed for the Adobe Corporation by Robert Slimbach, the fonts are based on types first cut by Claude Garamond (c. 1480–1561). Garamond was a pupil of Geoffroy Tory and is believed to have followed the Venetian models, although he introduced a number of important differences, and it is to him that we owe the letter we now know as "old style."

Printed and bound by Berryville Graphics

Designed by M. Kristen Bearse